SWITZERLAND TRAVEL GUIDE 2023 - 2024

A Comprehensive Pocket Guide To Switzerland: Unveiling The Swiss Gems With Complete Essential Tips & 7 Days Expert Itinerary For First Time Visitors

BY

William Jose

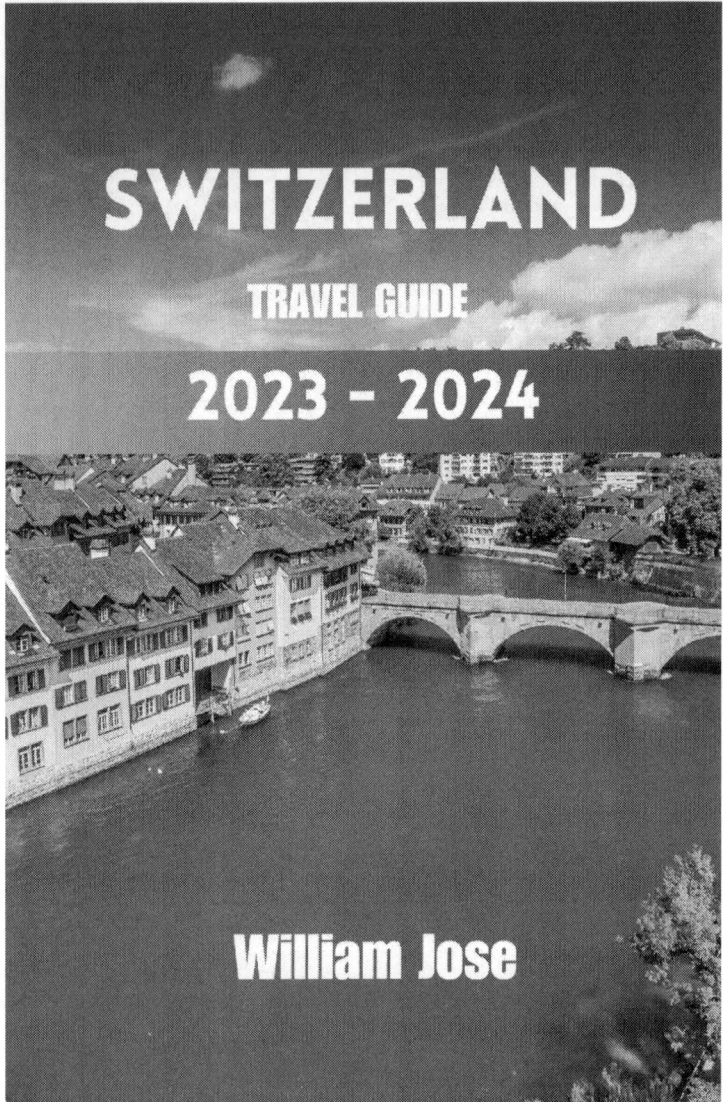

SWITZERLAND

TRAVEL GUIDE

2023 - 2024

William Jose

TABLE OF CONTENTS

INTRODUCTION

Switzerland, formally known as the Swiss Confederation, is a landlocked nation in Europe's center. Switzerland has become a worldwide emblem of stability and prosperity, thanks to its stunning scenery, political neutrality, and high quality of life.

Switzerland is geographically endowed with spectacular natural beauty. It is located among the beautiful Alps that dominate the country's southern and eastern areas. These snow-capped mountains not only provide breathtaking views, but also a variety of outdoor activities such as hiking, skiing, and climbing. Switzerland also has several beautiful lakes, such as Lake Geneva and Lake Zurich, which draw visitors from all over the globe.

The Swiss political system is distinguished by its unique direct democracy structure. The nation is split into 26 cantons, each having their own government and significant autonomy. Citizens have the right to vote in referendums and initiatives, ensuring that their opinions are heard on issues of national significance. Furthermore, since its last military action in 1815, Switzerland has stayed neutral in foreign wars, acquiring a reputation as a peace-loving country. Switzerland's finance and banking industry is one of its most identifiable aspects. Zurich and Geneva are well-known as significant worldwide financial centers, with a plethora of multinational banks and financial organizations. A highly qualified workforce, technical innovation, and a significant concentration on precision engineering, medicines, and high-end timepieces underpin the country's robust economy. Swiss corporations like Nestlé, Novartis, and Rolex are known across the globe for their excellence and quality.

Switzerland's four national languages, German, French, Italian, and Romansh, form a cultural mosaic. This linguistic variety is mirrored in the country's rich literary, artistic, and culinary past. Swiss cuisine is a lovely combination of adjacent country influences, including delicacies such as fondue, raclette, and chocolate.

The Swiss transportation system is well-known for its dependability and timeliness. The nation has an extensive network of railways, trams, and buses that allow visitors to easily tour its many areas. Furthermore, Switzerland's well-maintained road infrastructure and well-marked hiking routes allow tourists to get up close and personal with the country's natural treasures.

Finally, Switzerland is an enthralling nation that combines natural beauty, political stability, and economic success. Its devotion to democracy, impartial position, and great quality of life make it both a popular tourist destination and a desirable place to live. Switzerland guarantees a wonderful experience for those who come, whether exploring its snow-covered peaks, immersing themselves in its dynamic cities, or tasting its gastronomic pleasures.

Brief History of Switzerland

Switzerland is a tiny landlocked nation in the middle of Europe, formally known as the Swiss Confederation. Its distinct past is inextricably linked to the evolution of European civilisation and the battle for independence and neutrality.

Switzerland's beginnings may be traced back to the late medieval period, when numerous cantons, or districts, in the Swiss Alps created the Swiss Confederation in 1291. As more cantons joined the union, the confederation increased in size and importance throughout the ages.

During the Renaissance, art, literature, and science flourished in Switzerland. It did, however, suffer various hurdles, including religious strife. The Swiss Reformation in the 16th century resulted in internal turmoil due to the divide of Protestant and Catholic cantons.

Switzerland saw a surge of political and social upheavals in the nineteenth century. In 1848, the nation enacted a federal constitution, which established a more centralized administration while maintaining a high level of cantonal autonomy. To this day, the federal structure is a distinctive characteristic of Switzerland's political system. Switzerland was able to preserve its independence throughout Europe's stormy past, including both World Wars. It has a long history of neutrality, which has contributed to its stability and reputation as an international crisis mediator.

Switzerland's economy has prospered throughout the years, owing to a robust industrial sector that includes precise instruments, equipment, medicines, and timepieces. Switzerland has also emerged as a worldwide financial and banking powerhouse, with cities such as Zurich and Geneva playing important roles in the financial world.

Switzerland is known for its direct democracy, which allows residents to participate in decision-making via referendums and initiatives. This structure has promoted political stability and increased public participation. Switzerland is also noted for its dedication to international diplomacy and humanitarian activities. It is home to a number of international organizations, notably the Red Cross, and actively participates in global peacekeeping efforts.

Today, Switzerland is an affluent and peaceful country known for its political stability, excellent quality of life, and strong dedication to human rights. Its rich history and cultural variety continue to form its distinct character as a European crossroads nation.

Switzerland's Population And People

Switzerland is a tiny landlocked nation in central Europe with a population of around 8.6 million people. Switzerland, despite its small size, has a rich and diversified cultural legacy, making it a popular tourist destination. The Swiss hotel business is known for providing world-class service and paying close attention to detail.

Visitors from all over the world come to see the country's beautiful scenery, which include the majestic Alps, gorgeous lakes, and lovely villages. Switzerland is well-known for its ski resorts, hiking routes, and outdoor sports, making it a great destination for thrill seekers. Furthermore, the nation provides a wealth of cultural experiences, ranging from historical sites to art institutions and music festivals.

Swiss hospitality is distinguished by its professionalism, efficiency, and kindness. Switzerland's hotels, restaurants, and resorts try to give visitors an exceptional experience by providing first-rate facilities, superb food, and personalized service. The Swiss take pleasure in their reputation for hospitality, making guests feel welcome and well-cared for throughout their visit. Overall, the Swiss population contributes to the country's thriving hospitality industry, combining Swiss precision with kindness to offer an unforgettable experience for travelers discovering the country's natural beauty and cultural assets.

Religious Belief in Switzerland

Switzerland is noted for its religious tolerance and cultural variety. The nation has a rich religious history, with diverse religions coexisting harmoniously. Switzerland's prevalent religion is Christianity, with the vast majority of the people identifying as Roman Catholic or Protestant.

Roman Catholicism has extensive roots in Switzerland, particularly in the west and south. With many churches and religious institutions distributed over the nation, the Catholic Church plays an important role in the religious and social life of its faithful. Protestantism, particularly the Reformed strain, is also extensively practiced in Switzerland, notably in the middle and northern regions. The Swiss Reformed Church is the country's biggest Protestant denomination.

Switzerland has religious groups other than Christianity, such as Islam, Judaism, and Buddhism. Islam has grown dramatically in recent years, owing mostly to immigration from Muslim-majority nations. Mosques and Islamic institutions have been built to meet the requirements of the Muslim community.

Switzerland also boasts a small but dynamic Jewish population, centered mostly in Zurich, Geneva, and Basel. Synagogues and Jewish cultural organizations serve as meeting places for religious observance and communal events.

Buddhism is becoming more popular in Switzerland, with several Buddhist centers and temples providing meditation training and lectures. Other religious communities, such as Hindus and Sikhs, have temples throughout the nation as well.

Overall, Switzerland values religious freedom and respects its citizens' different religious views. The Swiss constitution provides religious freedom, enabling people to practice their beliefs freely and peacefully. This diversified and inclusive attitude has helped Switzerland establish a reputation as a society that appreciates religious plurality and peace.

Chapter One

Getting To Switzerland, The Tourist Paradise

Traveling to Switzerland is a wonderful experience full of pleasant joy. The breathtaking magnificence of the Swiss Alps inspires awe and astonishment. Your pulse beats faster as you drive through the lovely scenery. The fresh mountain air awakens your senses, while the lush green meadows and crystal-clear lakes provide a relaxing environment. Every minute is filled with fun and adventure, whether you're skiing down snow-capped slopes or wandering through picturesque Swiss towns. The Swiss people's warm welcome adds a lovely touch to your holiday, making it an amazing voyage of exploration and relaxation.

The Cost of Air Travel To Switzerland

The cost and availability of air travel to Switzerland from various regions might vary based on the airline, time of year, and other considerations. Here are some typical flight times and prices from prominent international airports to Switzerland:

Airport Zurich (ZRH):

Flight length is around 1.5 hours, and costs vary from $50 to $300, depending on the airline and booking period.

Flight time from New York City is usually 7-8 hours, with airfares ranging from $400 to $1,200 depending on the carrier and season.

Flight time from Dubai, United Arab Emirates is around 6 hours, and airfares vary from $400 to $1,000, depending on the airline and booking period.

Geneva International Airport (GVA):

Flight time from Paris is around one hour, and costs vary from $50 to $200, depending on the airline and booking time.

Flights from Berlin, Germany, take around 1.5 hours and cost between $70 and $250, depending on the carrier and season.

Flight time from Istanbul, Turkey is around 3 hours, and costs vary from $150 to $400, depending on the airline and booking period.

The Cost of land Travel To Switzerland

Traveling to Switzerland by land from other countries may be accomplished via a variety of modes of transportation, including trains, buses, and private vehicles. The expenses will vary based on the distance traveled, form of transportation used, and individual preferences. Here's a broad summary of land travel possibilities from surrounding countries to Switzerland, along with projected costs:

Germany:

Rail: Direct rail connections exist between major German cities and Swiss cities such as Zurich, Basel, and Geneva. The price is determined on the departure city and class of travel. A second-class ticket from Munich to Zurich, for example, might cost between €60 and €80 ($70 and $90).

Bus: Long-distance buses such as FlixBus provide cost-effective solutions. A one-way trip from German cities to Swiss locations might cost between €20 and €40 ($23 and $46).

France:

Train: TGV trains link Paris to Geneva, Basel, and Zurich. The price varies according to the class and booking time. A second-class ticket from Paris to Geneva might cost between €60 and €100 ($70 and 115).

Driving from France to Switzerland by car is a possibility, although it incurs tolls and fuel expenditures. The annual toll (vignette) on Swiss roadways is roughly CHF 40 ($44).

Italy:

Rail: Direct rail connections exist between major Italian cities and Swiss cities such as Zurich, Geneva, and Lugano. The price is determined on the departure city and class of travel. A second-class ticket from Milan to Zurich may cost between €50 and €80 ($58 and $92).

Driving from Italy to Switzerland is doable, however tolls and fuel expenses may apply. The Swiss vignette is necessary to drive on Swiss roadways.

Austria:

Train: Direct trains link Austrian cities such as Vienna, Innsbruck, and Salzburg with towns in Switzerland. Prices vary according to departure city and class of travel. A second-class ticket from Vienna to Zurich, for example, might cost between €80 and €100 ($92-115).

Driving from Austria to Switzerland is a possibility, however tolls and fuel expenses may apply. The Swiss vignette is necessary to drive on Swiss roadways.

Liechtenstein:

Railway: Because Liechtenstein is a tiny nation, it lacks its own railway system. However, trains from adjacent Swiss towns such as Zurich or Buchs in eastern Switzerland may take you to Liechtenstein.

Driving to Liechtenstein from Switzerland is simple and does not need a vignette.

It's crucial to remember that these are anticipated prices that might alter depending on things like travel class, booking time, and currency rates. It's always a good idea to double-check with individual transportation companies for the most up-to-date prices and alternatives.

Sea Travel To Switzerland

Switzerland is a landlocked nation in the center of Europe, which means it lacks direct access to the sea. Traveling to Switzerland by water is still conceivable, albeit it would need extra transit such as trains, buses, or aircraft. Here are a few marine travel possibilities from various areas to Switzerland:

Traveling by sea from a European port to a neighboring country:

If you live near a European port, you may take a cruise or ferry to a nearby nation like Italy, France, or Germany, and then continue your trip by land to Switzerland. Once at the harbor, you may go to Switzerland by rail or bus. The cost of this option would be determined by the cruise or ferry operator you pick, as well as the form of transportation you choose afterwards.

Traveling by Sea from North America to Europe: If you are in North America, you may take a transatlantic cruise to a European port. You may then take ground transit to Switzerland. Transatlantic cruises vary in length, facilities, and cost, so it's vital to shop around to find one that fits your needs and budget. Consider the cost of land transportation to Switzerland, which may include train or plane tickets.

Sea Travel from Other Continents to Europe: If you live on another continent, such as Asia or Australia, you may take a cruise or ship journey to a European port. After arriving in Europe, you may travel by land to Switzerland. The pricing and availability of these cruises might vary greatly based on your location, the cruise company, and the season.

Due to the country's landlocked geography, going to Switzerland by water is not the most straightforward or usual alternative. Most visitors choose to go to Switzerland by air or by ground transportation such as trains or buses. These modes of transportation provide more ease, efficiency, and direct access to Swiss cities.

Costs vary widely based on criteria such as your location, the form of sea transportation selected, the time of year, the cruise company, and any extra land transit fees. To establish the entire cost of your trip to Switzerland, it is essential that you investigate individual cruise alternatives, compare pricing, and consider other travel fees.

Month by Month Weather in Switzerland

January - February

Switzerland has winter weather in January and February, with chilly temperatures and snowfall. In the lowlands, average temperatures vary from -2°C to 5°C (28°F to 41°F), whereas in the mountains, temperatures may plummet below freezing, often reaching -10°C (14°F) or below. During this time of year, snowfall is frequent throughout the country, producing a stunning winter wonderland. The quantity of snowfall varies based on location, with the Alps receiving the most. It is best to dress warmly and be prepared for ice weather, particularly at higher altitudes. During this period, indoor activities such as visiting museums or tasting Swiss cuisine are popular.

March - April

Switzerland transitions from winter to spring between March and April. During this time, the weather might change dramatically. Colder temperatures predominate in March, particularly at higher elevations, with average highs ranging from 3°C to 10°C (37°F to 50°F). Snowfall is still likely, particularly in mountainous areas. Temperatures in April are warmer, with typical highs ranging from 10°C to 16°C (50°F to 61°F). The snow starts to melt, revealing blooming landscapes. However, rain showers are usual at this time of year, and weather patterns might shift. It is best to dress in layers and be prepared for both cold and warm weather.

May - June

Switzerland transitions from spring to early summer between May and June. During this time, the weather progressively turns softer and warmer. Temperatures in May range from 10 to 20 degrees Celsius (50 to 68 degrees Fahrenheit), with occasional rains. Temperatures climb to an average of 15 to 25 degrees Celsius (59 to 77 degrees Fahrenheit) in June, and the days are longer and brighter. It's an excellent time to discover Switzerland's stunning landscapes and engage in outdoor activities.

July - August

July and August in Switzerland feature good summer weather with moderate to warm temperatures and typically sunny circumstances. Temperatures at this time usually between 20°C (68°F) and 25°C (77°F), but may infrequently reach higher levels, particularly in low-lying areas. It's a great season for outdoor activities like hiking, riding, and experiencing the beautiful Swiss landscapes. The days are long, with enough light to explore the stunning countryside. It should be noted, however, that weather in Switzerland may vary depending on geography and altitude. Temperatures in higher alpine locations may be colder, and rain showers or thunderstorms are likely. Pack a variety of summer apparel and layers to account for anticipated temperature swings.

September - October

September to October in Switzerland represents the shift from summer to autumn. The weather steadily cools down throughout this period as the days get shorter. Temperatures in September vary from 10°C to 20°C (50°F to 68°F), with some rain. Temperatures decrease further in October, averaging from 5°C to 15°C (41°F to 59°F). Autumn leaves colors begin to emerge, creating a beautiful environment. It is best to bring layers of clothes to handle shifting temperatures and to be prepared for a variety of weather situations, including sunny days and rain showers.

November - December

The changeover from November to December in Switzerland results in noteworthy variations in meteorological conditions. Temperatures progressively decrease as the nation enters late October and approaches winter, and the landscapes turn into a stunning winter wonderland. In November, average temperatures in lower locations vary from 3°C to 10°C (37°F to 50°F), whereas temperatures in higher altitudes are cooler. Rainfall is frequent, and snow may begin to fall in mountainous locations, particularly at higher elevations. As December approaches, the frost deepens and temperatures drop even farther. Temperatures in lower locations vary from -2°C to 5°C (28°F to 41°F), while temperatures in higher altitudes are sub-zero. Snowfall becomes increasingly common, blanketing the Alps and adjacent areas. Ski resorts anticipate the first snow falls with bated breath, drawing winter sports lovers from all over the globe. The onset of winter in Switzerland marks the change from November to December, with cooler temperatures and the breathtaking splendor of snow-covered landscapes setting the scene for the impending holiday season.

Chapter Two

Swiss Travel Preparation

Preparation is the key to having a stress-free trip in Switzerland. From packing the correct gear to researching sites and knowing local traditions, comprehensive planning ensures that you make the most of your trip and leave with great memories in the middle of Switzerland's stunning beauty.

Best Time To Visit Switzerland

The ideal time to visit Iceland is determined by your choices and what you want to see and do. The summer months of June through August are perfect for pleasant weather, vivid sceneries, and extended daylight hours. You may enjoy nice temperatures ranging from 10°C to 20°C (50°F to 68°F), tour the famed Golden Circle, see gorgeous waterfalls, and even go trekking or camping during this period.

If, on the other hand, you want to see the enchanting Northern Lights, the winter months of November to February are the greatest time. Despite the low temperatures ranging from -1°C to 5°C (30°F to 41°F), the Aurora Borealis may be seen lighting up the night sky.

Spring (March to May) and fall (September to October) provide a balance between the two extremes, with fewer people, milder temperatures, and chances to see both the Northern Lights and Iceland's distinctive landscapes.

Finally, whether you want to see the midnight sun or the Northern Lights, the ideal time to visit Iceland depends on your choices.

Switzerland Neighborhoods City Tour

Switzerland is well-known for its beautiful scenery, lovely towns, and well-preserved neighborhoods. Here's a look at some of Switzerland's most prominent neighborhoods:

Zurich's Old Town (Altstadt): Begin your journey at the heart of Zurich, Switzerland's biggest city. The Old Town is a historic district with winding lanes, ancient architecture, and a lively ambiance. Visit the famed Bahnhofstrasse, a well-known retail strip, and sights like the Grossmünster and Fraumünster churches.

Les Pâquis, Geneva: Visit Geneva, an international metropolis noted for its diplomacy and the beautiful Lake Geneva. Les Pâquis is a diversified area near the lake that offers a bustling ambiance with contemporary cafés, restaurants, and a thriving nightlife. Enjoy breathtaking views of the Jet d'Eau, Geneva's famed water fountain, while strolling along the lakeside promenade.

Lausanne Old Town: Travel to Lausanne, a lovely city on Lake Geneva. The Old Town of Lausanne, also known as Cité, is located on a hill and has small, winding alleyways, medieval buildings, and attractive squares. Explore the old neighborhood's small boutiques and cafés as well as the spectacular Lausanne Cathedral.

Bern's Altstadt is well-known for its well-preserved medieval old town, which is a UNESCO World Heritage site. Stroll around the Altstadt and marvel at the unique arcades, sandstone façade, and the Zytglogge clock tower. Don't miss Bear Park, where you may observe the city's icon, bears, in their natural environment.

St. Alban, Basel: Explore the St. Alban area in Basel, a city known for its art and culture. This vibrant neighborhood is

Packed with magnificently restored medieval buildings, cobblestone streets, and a bohemian vibe. Visit the Museum Tinguely, which is devoted to the works of Swiss artist Jean Tinguely, and explore the attractive cafés, art shops, and boutiques.

Geneva's Old Town (Vieille Ville): Return to Geneva and tour the city's own Old Town, Vieille Ville. This medieval district is a labyrinth of winding alleyways, secret courtyards, and lovely squares. Explore St. Peter's Cathedral, the Maison Tavel (Geneva's oldest residence, now a museum), and the Place du Bourg-de-Four, a busy square lined by cafés and restaurants.

These are just a handful of the many charming neighborhoods to discover in Switzerland's cities. Each has its own distinct charm, history, and attractions, making for a fascinating cultural experience. Have fun on your city tour!

Transit Means of Exploring the Neighborhood

Switzerland has a number of transportation choices for touring its neighboring cities. Here are some examples of popular modes of transportation:

Trains: Switzerland boasts a vast and efficient rail network that is often recognized as one of the finest in the world. The bulk of rail services in Switzerland are operated by Swiss Federal Railways (SBB), which connects major cities and communities across the nation. Trains are dependable, on time, and provide breathtaking vistas of the Swiss environment.

Trams and buses: Trams and buses are prominent forms of urban and suburban transportation. Swiss towns such as Zurich, Geneva, Basel, and Bern offer outstanding tram and bus networks that provide for easy access to a variety of districts and attractions. These services are often well-connected and operate on a regular basis.

Switzerland has numerous lovely lakes, including Lake Geneva, Lake Zurich, Lake Lucerne, and Lake Thun. Many towns and communities are situated on the shores of these lakes, which may be explored by ferry or boat. These picturesque boats provide a unique opportunity to see Swiss scenery while commuting between places.

Cable Cars and Funiculars: Switzerland is well-known for its breathtaking alpine landscapes, and cable cars and funiculars are often utilized to reach hilly locations. These modes of transportation may take you to spectacular vistas, ski resorts, hiking routes, and beautiful mountain communities. Cable car networks are well-known in towns such as Zermatt, Interlaken, and Lucerne.

Renting a vehicle is an alternative if you desire more freedom and independence. Switzerland's road system is well-maintained, and traveling about the nation is a simple way to discover its districts. However, bear in mind that certain cities have restricted traffic zones or limited parking, so verify the restrictions ahead of time.

Bicycles: Switzerland is a bicycle-friendly country, with dedicated bike lanes and rental services in many cities. You may hire bicycles and ride around communities at your leisure. Cycling is an excellent way to take in the scenery and learn about the local culture.

It's worth mentioning that Switzerland offers an extensive and integrated public transportation system that allows you to smoothly mix various types of transportation. The Swiss Travel Pass is a popular choice for travelers, since it provides unrestricted travel on trains, buses, and boats for a certain period of time. Plan your trip ahead of time and consider

It's worth noting that Switzerland is not a member of the European Union, but it is a member of the Schengen Area, which allows for free travel among select European nations. As a result, Switzerland's admission restrictions are often linked with Schengen standards.

Stay Duration

The length of a tourist's stay in Switzerland varies according to personal tastes, available vacation time, and planned activities. Switzerland has a wide variety of attractions, ranging from magnificent scenery to dynamic towns, which might impact the duration of a visit.

A journey of 7 to 14 days is typically advised for a thorough tour that enables you to see several places and participate in various activities. This timetable enables you to visit renowned tourist locations such as Zurich, Lucerne, Geneva, Interlaken, and the Swiss Alps.

If you have limited time, a 3- to 5-day trip might nevertheless give you a taste of Switzerland's attractions. For example, you may spend time investigating a single region or city in detail, such as Zurich and its neighboring territories.

Finally, the length of your stay in Switzerland is determined by your particular interests, travel objectives, and the amount of time you have available. It's essential to think about things like transportation between places, the time necessary for various activities (hiking, skiing, museum visits, etc.), and your preferred travel speed.

Switzerland Travel Essentials

When preparing for a vacation to Switzerland, consider the weather and the activities you want to participate in. Here's a list of things you should bring on your trip:

Clothing:

Warm layers: Because temperatures in Switzerland may fluctuate, bring lightweight sweaters, long-sleeved shirts, and a couple thicker layers, such as a fleece or a light jacket.

Waterproof jacket: Although Switzerland is famed for its gorgeous scenery, rain showers are possible. To remain dry, bring a waterproof or water-resistant jacket.

strolling shoes that are comfortable: Switzerland has numerous options for hiking and strolling. Pack shoes that are appropriate for the terrain.

Hat, gloves, and scarf: These items can keep you warm if you're traveling during the winter months or going to higher heights.

Travel documentation:

Passport: Check that your passport is valid for at least six months beyond the duration of your anticipated stay.

Check your nationality to see whether you need a visa to enter Switzerland.

Travel insurance: Having travel insurance that covers medical emergencies, trip cancellation, and lost possessions is always a smart idea.

Carry printed copies of your vacation itinerary, hotel reservations, and crucial contact information.

Accessories and electronics:

Adapter plug: Switzerland uses a kind J connector, therefore carry an adapter if your electronics use another kind of plug.

With a competent camera, you may capture the breathtaking Swiss landscapes and cityscapes.

Keep your gadgets charged while touring with a portable charger.

Items for personal care:

Amenities: Bring travel-sized amenities such as toothpaste, toothbrushes, shampoo, conditioner, and any other personal care things you may need.

Medications: If you need prescription medicine, carry enough for the length of your vacation.

Sunscreen: Even if you travel during the cooler months, the sun's rays may be intense, particularly at higher elevations.

Miscellaneous:

A travel handbook may give useful information on the country's attractions, history, and culture.

Travel funds: Bring Swiss Francs (CHF) or a dependable mechanism to access cash in Switzerland, such as a credit or debit card.

Daypack: A tiny backpack or daypack is useful for carrying items on day travels.

Check the weather prediction for the individual areas of Switzerland you want to visit and update your packing list appropriately. Consider any special activities you'll be doing, such as skiing or swimming, and bring the proper equipment.

Chapter Three

Top Attractions And Recreational Activities in Switzerland

Switzerland, a nation of spectacular beauty, provides a tapestry of sights and attractions that enchant the senses and move the emotions. This fascinating nation invites tourists with its incomparable beauty and many recreational activities, from the magnificent Swiss Alps to the peaceful lakes and attractive towns. Switzerland offers a symphony of experiences that will leave you enthralled and craving for more, whether you find yourself gazing in amazement at towering peaks, discovering old castles, or engaging on exhilarating outdoor excursions.

Switzerland Top Attractions You Must Not Miss

Switzerland is well-known for its beautiful scenery, lovely towns, and outdoor activities. Here are some of Switzerland's best attractions:

Matterhorn: This majestic peak in the Swiss Alps is one of Switzerland's most renowned sights. It has beautiful vistas and is a popular hiking, skiing, and climbing destination.

Lake Geneva is the biggest lake in Western Europe, located on the border between Switzerland and France. On its banks, the towns of Geneva, Lausanne, and Montreux provide breathtaking landscapes, historic buildings, and cultural attractions.

Jungfraujoch: Also known as the "Top of Europe," Jungfraujoch is Europe's highest railway station, standing at 3,454 meters (11,332 feet). It has an Ice Palace, Sphinx Observatory, and hiking routes, as well as panoramic views of the neighboring Bernese Alps.

Lucerne is a lovely city on the banks of Lake Lucerne that is surrounded by mountains. It has a well-preserved medieval old town, a renowned wooden Chapel Bridge (Kapellbrücke), and a number of cultural treasures, including the Lion Monument.

Zurich: Zurich, Switzerland's biggest city, mixes modernism and ancient appeal. It has a thriving arts scene, world-class museums, expensive retail areas, and a lovely old town complete with cobblestone lanes and medieval buildings.

Bern: Switzerland's capital, Bern, is a UNESCO World Heritage Site due to its well-preserved medieval old town. Bern is famous for its Bear Park, Federal Palace, Clock Tower, and Bern Cathedral.

Zermatt is a car-free Alpine resort that is a haven for outdoor lovers, particularly skiers and snowboarders. Zermatt has fantastic skiing, breathtaking views of the Matterhorn, and a delightful town vibe.

Interlaken: Interlaken is a famous base for outdoor activities in the Jungfrau area, nestled between two magnificent lakes. It provides convenient access to Jungfraujoch and neighboring hiking routes, as well as a broad selection of adventure activities such as paragliding, skydiving, and canyoning.

Chillon Castle: Located near Montreux on the banks of Lake Geneva, Chillon Castle is a well-preserved medieval fortification dating back to the 12th century. It's one of the most visited medieval places in Switzerland, with guided tours and spectacular lake views.

Rhine Falls: The Rhine Falls, located near the town of Schaffhausen, is Europe's biggest waterfall. Visitors may get up close and personal with the falls by taking boat tours or strolling over the observation decks.

These are just a handful of the numerous attractions available in Switzerland. Switzerland offers something for everyone, whether you're looking for natural beauty, cultural activities, or outdoor adventures.

Who Should Visit Switzerland?

Switzerland is a lovely country with a broad choice of sights and experiences, making it a perfect destination for many sorts of visitors. Here are some examples of persons who would appreciate visiting Switzerland:

Nature and adventure enthusiasts will enjoy Switzerland's beautiful landscapes, which include the Swiss Alps, lovely lakes, and attractive towns. It is ideal for hiking, skiing, snowboarding, climbing, and other outdoor sports.

Culture and History Buffs: Switzerland has a great history and a rich cultural heritage. Visitors who want to visit ancient villages, historic castles, museums, and traditional Swiss traditions will have much to do.

Train and scenic route enthusiasts will enjoy Switzerland's efficient and picturesque train network. Train enthusiasts will be charmed by the Swiss rail system, which provides beautiful vistas of mountains, valleys, and lakes.

Food and Wine Lovers: Switzerland is well-known for its delectable chocolates, cheeses, and other culinary treats. Fondue, raclette, and Swiss wines are among the many Swiss delicacies available to food and wine enthusiasts.

Seekers of Adventure Sports: Switzerland is a sanctuary for those interested in adventure sports. There are several adrenaline-pumping things to attempt, ranging from paragliding and skydiving to canyoning and bungee jumping.

Families: Switzerland is a family-friendly destination with a variety of kid-friendly attractions such as interactive museums, theme parks, and nature parks. Outdoor activities for families in the lovely Swiss countryside include boating, cycling, and picnics.

Elegance Travelers: Switzerland is known for its elegance and refinement. Those looking for a lavish and pampered holiday will find exclusive resorts, exquisite restaurants, high-end shopping, and world-class spas.

Winter Sports Enthusiasts: Switzerland is a renowned winter sports destination. Its world-class ski resorts, including Zermatt, Verbier, and St. Moritz, provides superb slopes, well-kept paths, and a range of winter sports like snowboarding, ice climbing, and ice skating.

Photographers: With its gorgeous scenery, attractive villages, and lovely lakes, Switzerland offers plenty of opportunities for spectacular photography. Photographers will discover a plethora of interesting themes, ranging from snow-capped peaks and alpine meadows to colorful lakeside settlements.

Seekers of Wellness & Spa getaways: Switzerland is well-known for its wellness resorts and spa getaways. Thermal baths, health treatments, and deluxe spa experiences in gorgeous surroundings are available to visitors wishing to rest and revitalize.

Attendees at Music Festivals: Throughout the year, Switzerland holds a variety of music festivals, ranging from classical music and opera festivals to jazz and current music events. Music fans may experience world-class performances in breathtaking settings.

It is crucial to remember that these are broad recommendations, and Switzerland might appeal to a diverse spectrum of people. Finally, everybody who enjoys breathtaking natural beauty, outdoor activities, rich history, and cultural experiences can find something to love in Switzerland.

Top Adventure Fun Activities

Switzerland is well-known for its beautiful scenery and outdoor activities. Here are some of the top adventure activities in Switzerland for tourists:

Hiking: Switzerland has several hiking paths for people of all fitness levels. Hiking pathways such as the Haute Route, the Eiger Trail, and the Via Alpina provide stunning vistas of snow-capped peaks, glaciers, and scenic valleys in the Swiss Alps.

46

Skiing and snowboarding: Switzerland is a winter sports enthusiast's dream. The nation is home to world-class ski resorts including Zermatt, Verbier, St. Moritz, and Davos, which provide a variety of slopes for all ability levels. In the Swiss Alps, you may do downhill skiing, snowboarding, cross-country skiing, or even heli-skiing.

Paragliding: Experience the excitement of paragliding while admiring the breathtaking scenery of Switzerland. Paragliding is popular in Interlaken, Lucerne, and Engelberg, where you can fly into the air and experience a bird's-eye view of lakes, mountains, and attractive Swiss cities.

Canyoning: Canyoning activities allow you to explore Switzerland's stunning canyons. Descending waterfalls, sliding down natural rock slides, and leaping into crystal-clear pools are all part of this adventure sport. Canyoning is particularly popular in Interlaken, Ticino, and Grindelwald.

Biking & Mountain Biking: Switzerland has a wide network of on-road and off-road bicycle lanes, making it a cyclist's paradise. The surroundings of the nation are excellent for both relaxing bike rides and demanding mountain riding trips. The almost 3,000-kilometer Swiss National Bike Route is an excellent way to tour the nation on two wheels.

Whitewater Rafting: Put your skills to the test by whitewater rafting through Switzerland's rivers and rapids. The Lütschine River in Interlaken is a famous rafting destination, offering an adrenaline rush as you travel through spectacular rapids.

Glacier Trekking: Take a glacier trekking excursion to discover Switzerland's stunning glaciers. Hiking over ice fields, traversing crevasses, and discovering the spectacular ice formations of prominent glaciers such as the Aletsch Glacier and the Rhone Glacier are all possible with a qualified guide.

Skydiving: Take the leap of faith and experience the ultimate rush of skydiving in Switzerland. Interlaken is a well-known skydiving location, where you may jump out of an aircraft and freefall into the sky, soaking in beautiful vistas of the Swiss Alps.

These are just a handful of the exciting activities offered in Switzerland. Natural beauty and a well-developed tourist infrastructure make the country an attractive destination for outdoor lovers looking for exhilarating experiences.

Festivals and Events That Should Not be Missed

Throughout the year, Switzerland is recognized for its colorful festivals and events. Here are some festivals and events in Switzerland that you should not miss:

Basel Carnival (Basler Fasnacht): This three-day carnival, held in Basel in February or March, is one of the largest and most colorful in Switzerland. The streets are filled with music, parades, and festivals, and participants wear extravagant costumes and masks.

Montreux Jazz Festival: The Montreux Jazz Festival, held every July in Montreux, is one of the world's most recognized music events. It attracts music fans from all over the world with its wide roster of jazz, blues, rock, and pop musicians.

The Lucerne event is a well-known classical music event held in Lucerne. It is normally held in the summer, from August through September, and offers performances by globally renowned orchestras, conductors, and soloists.

The Zurich Street Parade is a major electronic music event that takes place in August. The parade is held in Zurich's streets, with colorful floats, DJs, and hundreds of people dancing to electronic rhythms.

The Fête de l'Escalade, held in December in Geneva, celebrates the city's triumph against an attempted invasion in 1602. A historical parade, torchlight processions, and traditional costumes are all part of the celebration. The smashing of a massive chocolate cauldron, representing the defeat of the invaders, is a highlight.

Locarno worldwide Film Festival: This prominent film festival, held in Locarno in August, features a diverse selection of worldwide films, including world premieres and avant-garde cinema. It draws well-known filmmakers, industry experts, and film fans.

Sechseläuten: Sechseläuten is a traditional spring event held on the third Monday of April in Zurich. The burning of the "Böögg," a snowman-shaped figure signifying winter, is the festival's climax. The shorter the summer is forecast to be, the quicker Böögg's head erupts in flames.

Lavaux Vineyard Terraces Open Days: The UNESCO World Heritage Site Lavaux Vineyard Terraces has open days in the spring and fall. Visitors may stroll through the scenic vineyards, sample local wines, and learn about the region's winemaking traditions.

These are just a handful of the numerous spectacular festivals and events held throughout Switzerland. The country's rich cultural history and gorgeous surroundings serve as an excellent background for these lively events.

Top Tourists Cities to Stay

Switzerland is well-known for its beautiful scenery, efficient infrastructure, and high standard of living. Here are some of the best cities in Switzerland to stay:

Zurich: As Switzerland's biggest city, Zurich provides a bustling urban experience that includes cultural attractions, great public transit, and a booming business landscape. It also has a charming ancient town and is located on the beaches of Lake Zurich.

51

Geneva: Located on the shores of Lake Geneva, Geneva is a worldwide diplomatic center and home to a number of international organizations. It boasts a diversified population, a rich history, and a great quality of life. The city is well-known for its natural beauty, high-end shopping, and cultural activities.

Basel is noted for its medieval old town and strong art and cultural scene. It is located on the Rhine River. It is home to many notable museums, notably the Kunstmuseum Basel, as well as a plethora of pharmaceutical and chemical firms.

Bern: Bern, Switzerland's capital, has a lovely medieval old town that is a UNESCO World Heritage site. The city is well-known for its well-preserved arcades, historical attractions including Bear Park, and the unique Zytglogge clock tower.

Lucerne: This attractive city is a renowned tourist destination, nestled among gorgeous alpine scenery and located on the banks of Lake Lucerne. Lucerne is famous for its well-preserved medieval architecture, the Chapel Bridge, and its closeness to the spectacular Swiss Alps.

Lausanne is a dynamic city on the banks of Lake Geneva recognized for its young vitality and strong cultural scene. It houses the International Olympic Committee's headquarters and has excellent views of the lake and adjacent vineyards.

Interlaken: Interlaken, located in the heart of the Swiss Alps, is a haven for outdoor enthusiasts. It is surrounded by magnificent mountains and provides a gateway to famous attractions like the Jungfrau, Schilthorn, and Aletsch Glacier. Hiking, skiing, and paragliding are all popular activities.

These cities have a variety of activities, superb facilities, and easy access to the natural beauty of Switzerland. The greatest city to stay in is determined by your interests, lifestyle, and the purpose of your vacation.

Chapter Four

Switzerland Historical Monuments And Art Galleries

Switzerland, a time capsule, proudly maintains its legacy in the shape of beautiful historical sites, where echoes of the past blend with the beauty of the present.

Swiss Historical Monuments

Switzerland is well-known for its rich legacy and historical monuments, as well as its numerous cultural and architectural treasures. Here are a few noteworthy examples:

Chillon Castle is one of Switzerland's most visited historic landmarks, located on the banks of Lake Geneva near Montreux. It comes from the 12th century and provides breathtaking views of the lake and neighboring mountains.

The Old Town of Bern: The Old Town of Bern, Switzerland's capital city, is a UNESCO World Heritage site. It's famous for its well-preserved medieval architecture, which includes the Zytglogge (Clock Tower), Bern Cathedral, and many cobblestone streets and arcades.

Bellinzona Castles: The three castles of Bellinzona are another UNESCO World Heritage site, situated in the Italian-speaking canton of Ticino. These well-preserved medieval fortresses were strategically placed to control the Alpine passes.

Lavaux Vineyards: The Lavaux Vineyards are a UNESCO World Heritage property located on the shores of Lake Geneva. This terraced grape area goes back to the 11th century and provides stunning views of the lake and neighboring Alps.

Aletsch Glacier: Located in the Swiss Alps, the Aletsch Glacier is the biggest glacier in the Alps and a UNESCO World Heritage site. It spans over 23 kilometers and is surrounded by stunning peaks and alpine scenery.

The Matterhorn: Although not a typical historical monument, the Matterhorn is one of the world's most recognizable mountains. It is generally connected with Switzerland and is a popular destination for mountaineers and visitors. It is located in the Swiss Alps.

St. Peter's Cathedral, Geneva: St. Peter's Cathedral is a well-known landmark in Geneva. It was built in the 12th century and is notable for its eclectic combination of architectural styles, including Gothic and Romanesque.

These are only a few examples of Switzerland's cultural and historical monuments. Many more breathtaking places exhibit the country's rich cultural and historical legacy.

Contemporary Art And Galleries Museums

Switzerland has a thriving art culture including various modern art galleries and museums. Here are a few important ones to look into:

Kunsthaus Zürich (Zürich): The Kunsthaus Zürich is one of Switzerland's major art museums, with a broad collection of modern and contemporary art. It has paintings by notable painters such as Picasso, Monet, Chagall, and many more.

Fondation Beyeler (Riehen/Basel): Fondation Beyeler is a notable art museum specializing in modern and contemporary art. It contains an extraordinary collection of works by Rothko, Warhol, Lichtenstein, and Bacon.

Museum of Contemporary Art (Basel): The Kunstmuseum Basel Gegenwart is a museum devoted to contemporary art from the 1960s to the present. It features works by known and new artists, as well as a variety of media and aesthetic styles.

Kunsthalle Basel (Basel) is a contemporary art institution that hosts temporary exhibits and projects by national and international artists. It is well-known for its experimental and forward-thinking approach to modern art.

Museum Tinguely (Basel): The Museum Tinguely is devoted to the works of Swiss artist Jean Tinguely, who is best known for his kinetic art sculptures. The museum has a large collection of Tinguely's work as well as temporary exhibits of other contemporary artists.

Migros Museum für Gegenwartskunst (Zürich): The Migros Museum for Contemporary Art is a major contemporary art institution in Zurich. It promotes creative and experimental art practices by showcasing temporary exhibits and initiatives by national and international artists.

Kunstmuseum Bern (Bern): One of Switzerland's oldest art museums, the Kunstmuseum Bern has a substantial collection of modern and contemporary art. It features changing exhibits highlighting different aesthetic trends and artists.

Kunsthaus Baselland (Muttenz/Basel): Kunsthaus Baselland is a contemporary art center specializing in experimental and multidisciplinary works by rising artists. It encourages creative and thought-provoking approaches.

Aargauer Kunsthaus (Aarau): The Aargauer Kunsthaus is a modern art museum in Aarau. It offers a broad collection of modern and contemporary art, with a focus on Swiss artists.

These are only a handful of Switzerland's modern art galleries and museums. The nation boasts a diverse art scene, and there are many more galleries and organizations to visit around the country's many areas.

National Parks And Reserves

Switzerland features a number of protected areas and natural reserves worth visiting. Here are a few examples:

Swiss National Park: The Swiss National Park is the country's sole national park, located in the country's east. It was founded in 1914 and has an area of around 170 square kilometers (65 square miles). The park's vegetation and animals are diversified, including ibex, chamois, marmots, and golden eagles. Visitors may explore the park by trekking its various paths while adhering to its rigorous conservation guidelines.

Val Grande National Park: While nominally located in Italy, Val Grande shares a border with Switzerland and is readily accessible from the Swiss side. It is one of the Alps' biggest wilderness regions, comprising around 145 square kilometers (56 square miles). Val Grande is noted for its rocky terrain, deep valleys, and thick woods, which provide great hiking and nature exploring options.

Aletsch Glacier: Although not a typical national park, this UNESCO World Heritage site deserves to be included owing to its great ecological value. The Aletsch Glacier,

created by the surrounding mountains and crystal-clear water.

Chillon Castle, Montreux: Situated on the banks of Lake Geneva, Chillon Castle is a medieval fortification with breathtaking architecture and wonderful lake views. A guided tour of the castle is available, as is a walk along the lakeside promenade and a romantic lunch at one of the neighboring waterfront restaurants.

Giardini Estensi, Lugano: The Giardini Estensi, situated in southern Switzerland, is a lovely garden filled with exotic plants, flowers, and sculptures. The garden offers a tranquil and romantic setting in which to take a leisurely stroll, rest on the benches, and observe the natural beauty.

Before visiting these venues, be sure to verify the opening hours, seasonal availability, and any special criteria or limitations. Switzerland has many more romantic sites and gardens to discover depending on your interests and the area you want to visit.

Zoos And Educational Museums

Switzerland has a number of zoos and educational museums where visitors may learn about many areas of nature, science, and culture. Here are some of Switzerland's most prominent zoos and educational museums:

Zurich Zoo: Located in Zurich, the Zurich Zoo is one of Switzerland's most visited zoos. It is home to a diverse range of animals from throughout the globe and focuses on wildlife conservation and education.

Basel Zoo: The Basel Zoo, located in Basel, is Switzerland's oldest and biggest zoo. It has a wide animal collection, including exotic species, and offers educational programs and activities for visitors of all ages.

Papiliorama: Papiliorama is a one-of-a-kind tropical zoo in Kerzers. It is a butterfly, tropical plant, and nocturnal animal specialist. Indoor and outdoor displays, including a butterfly house and a nocturnal wildlife area, are available for visitors to explore.

Naturhistorisches Museum Basel: The Natural History Museum Basel has a large collection of natural history exhibits, such as fossils, minerals, and animal species. It provides a thorough picture of Earth's history and biodiversity.

Swiss Museum of Transport: The Swiss Museum of Transport, located in Lucerne, is an interactive museum devoted to different types of transportation, including trains, airplanes, vehicles, and more. It has many exhibitions, simulators, and vintage vehicles.

Geneva Museum of Natural History: The Geneva Museum of Natural History is well-known for its enormous collection of natural history specimens. It includes displays on anthropology, paleontology, geology, and zoology, providing visitors with a comprehensive look at the natural world.

Olympic Museum, Lausanne: For sports fans, the Olympic Museum in Lausanne is a fascinating excursion. It depicts the Olympic Games' history, Olympic athletes, and the principles connected with the Olympic movement.

Chaplin's World: Located in Corsier-sur-Vevey, Chaplin's World is a museum devoted to the famed comedian Charlie

Chaplin's life and career. It shows his personal life, cinematic career, and the renowned characters he created.

These are just a few examples of zoos and educational museums in Switzerland. Each institution provides a one-of-a-kind experience that combines entertainment and education to appeal to guests of all ages and interests.

Chapter Five

Eco-Friendly Accommodations in Switzerland And their Price Rates

Switzerland is well-known for its environmentally friendly lodgings that promote comfort, relaxation, and social amenities. These environmentally friendly hotels provide a variety of features to ensure that travelers have an enjoyable and sustainable stay. These lodgings, which range from lavish spas to tranquil natural settings, provide a refuge for relaxation and renewal.

Switzerland's environmentally friendly resorts and hotels promote sustainability by adopting energy-saving methods, harnessing renewable energy sources, and supporting eco-friendly projects. Organic food derived from local farms is available to guests, as are spa facilities that include natural and holistic therapies. Many lodgings also provide outdoor activities like hiking, cycling, and skiing, enabling tourists to immerse themselves in the stunning Swiss landscapes.

These eco-friendly hotels provide a feeling of community and social connection in addition to offering comfort and relaxation. The common spaces are intended to encourage visitors to interact with one another, creating a pleasant and inclusive environment. Communal eating rooms, lounges, and outdoor meeting places provide opportunities for visitors to make important relationships and share experiences.

Switzerland's eco-friendly lodgings provide the ideal balance of comfort, relaxation, and sustainable methods, guaranteeing that every visitor has an amazing and ecologically conscientious experience.

Tourist Hotels & Resorts on a Budget

Switzerland is well-known for its magnificent scenery, lovely towns, and excellent tourist infrastructure. It is, nevertheless, well-known for being an expensive vacation destination. Having said that, there are still several budget-friendly hotels and resorts in Switzerland that appeal to budget-conscious guests. Remember that even these possibilities may be more costly than budget lodgings in other countries. Here are a few recommendations:

Ibis Budget Zurich City West (Zurich): This hotel has low prices and is close to the city center. The nightly rate begins at $100.

Hotel Marta (Zurich): Hotel Marta is another budget-friendly alternative in Zurich, offering clean and pleasant rooms at moderate prices. The nightly rate begins at about $120.

Hotel Limmathof (Zurich): Located near the railway station, Hotel Limmathof provides affordable lodgings and easy access to public transit. The nightly rate begins at about $130.

Hotel Montana Zürich (Zurich): This hotel, located in the city center, provides reasonable prices and pleasant accommodations. The nightly rate begins at $150.

Hotel Bristol Zurich (Zurich): This hotel offers inexpensive lodging within walking distance to main attractions. The nightly rate begins at about $160.

Hotel ibis Lausanne Centre (Lausanne): This budget-friendly hotel in the center of Lausanne provides pleasant rooms at cheap prices. The nightly rate begins at about $120.

Hotel Crystal (Lucerne): Located in the city center of Lucerne, Hotel Crystal offers economical rooms with easy access to the major attractions. The nightly rate begins at $150.

Hotel Montana Zürich (Zurich): This hotel provides reasonable pricing and pleasant accommodations in a central location. The nightly rate begins at $150.

Hotel Welcome Inn (Kloten, near Zurich Airport): Hotel Welcome Inn is a fantastic alternative for a budget-friendly option near Zurich Airport. The nightly rate begins at $100.

These rates are estimates and may vary depending on the time of year, availability, and accommodation type. Check the most recent pricing and availability on hotel booking services or directly with the hotels themselves. Furthermore, bear in mind that the high cost of living in Switzerland extends to eating out and other costs, so plan appropriately for meals and activities throughout your stay.

Luxury Tourist Hotels & Resorts in Switzerland

Switzerland is well-known for its opulent hotels and resorts that provide spectacular vistas, first-rate service, and world-class facilities. Here are several well-known luxury hotels and resorts in Switzerland, along with estimated prices:

St. Moritz's Badrutt's Palace Hotel: This historic hotel in the center of St. Moritz provides luxury suites and spectacular mountain views. A regular double room begins at roughly $800 per night.

The Dolder Grand, Zurich: A five-star hotel famed for its exquisite accommodations, spa facilities, and Michelin-starred restaurants, The Dolder Grand is located in a tranquil position overlooking Zurich. Room prices start at about $700 per night.

Baur au Lac, Zurich: The famous Baur au Lac hotel is nestled in a serene park setting near Lake Zurich. It has magnificent accommodations, exquisite dining choices, and exceptional service. A regular double room begins at roughly $700 per night.

The Kulm Hotel in St. Moritz mixes heritage and modernity as one of the city's oldest hotels. It offers elegant accommodations, superb restaurants, and access to a variety of outdoor activities. Room prices start at about $600 per night.

Lucerne's Bürgenstock Hotels & Resort: Nestled high above Lake Lucerne, the Bürgenstock Resort provides spectacular vistas as well as a variety of exquisite lodgings, including the historic Bürgenstock Hotel. A basic double room begins at roughly $500 per night.

The Chedi Andermatt, Andermatt: This Swiss Alps five-star hotel mixes Alpine flair with Asian inspirations. It has magnificent accommodations, a large spa, and excellent eating choices. Room prices start at about $700 per night.

Vacation Rentals and Apartments

Switzerland has a diverse assortment of apartments and holiday rentals to accommodate a variety of budgets and interests. Apartment and vacation rental prices might vary based on location, size, amenities, and the time of year you want to stay. Following are some general guidelines:

Location: Rental costs in major cities like Zurich, Geneva, and Basel tend to be more than in smaller towns or rural regions. Prices may also be affected by proximity to tourist sites or natural features.

The size of the apartment or vacation rental will have a considerable influence on the cost. Larger lodgings with many bedrooms and living areas are usually more costly than smaller ones.

Apartments and holiday rentals with extra amenities such as parking, Wi-Fi, laundry facilities, swimming pools, or gyms are often more expensive.

Throughout the year, Switzerland is a popular tourist destination. Prices tend to be higher during busy tourist seasons such as summer (June to August) and winter (December to February). If you travel in the off-season, like spring or autumn, you may be able to locate more reasonable choices.

Stay length: Many vacation rentals offer discounts for longer stays, such as weekly or monthly rents. If you want to remain for a long amount of time, you may be able to negotiate a lower rate.

Here are some typical pricing ranges depending on the kind of lodging to give you a general sense of costs:

Budget options: In smaller cities or rural locations, you may be able to locate affordable flats or vacation rentals ranging from $80 to $150 per night.

Mid-range apartments or vacation rentals may cost from $150 to $300 per night in major tourist locations or bigger cities.

Luxury options: Depending on the location and exclusivity, upscale apartments or vacation rentals with premium facilities might cost $300 to $1,000 or more per night.

Please keep in mind that these are only estimates, and costs might vary greatly depending on the criteria indicated above. To get accurate and up-to-date price information for your preferred area and vacation dates, it is advised that you investigate individual rental websites or talk with travel agents or rental companies.

Swiss Hostels And Guesthouses

Switzerland has a wide range of guesthouses and hostels to suit all budgets and travel inclinations. The cost of lodging varies according on location, season, and amenities supplied. Here are some examples of Swiss guesthouses and hostels, along with their estimated costs:

Zurich Youth Hostel (Zurich): This contemporary hostel provides dormitory-style lodging with shared amenities. Prices per night vary from around CHF 40 to CHF 60.

Balmer's Hostel (Interlaken): Balmer's Hostel, located in the adventure-filled town of Interlaken, offers a dynamic environment with dormitory and private rooms. Prices begin at CHF 35 per night.

Geneva Hostel (Geneva): Geneva Hostel provides dormitory-style accommodations near Lake Geneva and within walking distance of the city center. Prices per night vary from around CHF 40 to CHF 60.

Alplodge (Lucerne): Alplodge is a low-cost hostel in the center of Lucerne. It offers both dormitory and individual rooms, with rates beginning at CHF 30 per night.

Balmers Herberge (Bern): Balmers Herberge is a prominent hostel in Bern's capital city that offers a variety of accommodation options, including dorms and individual rooms. Prices begin at CHF 35 per night.

Matterhorn Hostel (Zermatt): Matterhorn Hostel, located in the lovely town of Zermatt, offers economical lodging in dormitory-style rooms. Prices per night vary from around CHF 40 to CHF 60.

It is crucial to remember that these rates are estimates and may vary depending on accommodation type, season, and availability. Furthermore, some hostels may charge a fee for additional facilities or services.

Switzerland Tourist Camp Locations

Switzerland is a well-known tourist destination due to its beautiful scenery, lovely towns, and outdoor activities. While there are various campsites and venues around the nation, I'll highlight a few noteworthy ones as well as some basic pricing information. Prices may vary based on the season, location, and facilities supplied.

Jungfrau Camping (Lauterbrunnen): It is situated in the Bernese Oberland, surrounded by mountains and waterfalls. Provides a variety of lodging options, including tent pitches, caravan sites, and rental apartments.
A tent spot costs between CHF 40 and CHF 80 per night, depending on the season and location within the campground.

Interlaken Camping Manor Farm: Beautiful views of the Swiss Alps from this location near Lake Thun.
Rents out tent pitches, caravan spaces, and mobile homes.
Tent site prices range from around CHF 35 to CHF 55 per night, depending on the season and location within the campground.

TCS Solothurn Witi Camping (Solothurn): The lovely town of Solothurn, noted for its baroque architecture, is nearby.
Tent pitches, caravan spaces, and rented cabins are available.
Depending on the season, tent pitch costs vary from around CHF 25 to CHF 40 per night.

Jungwacht Camping (Thun): With beautiful lake and mountain views, this hotel is located on the beaches of Lake Thun.

Tent pitches, campervan parking, and rental units are available.

Prices for tent pitches range from around CHF 30 to CHF 50 per night, depending on the season and location within the campsite.

Zugersee Camping (Zug): Located beside Lake Zug, this hotel provides a pleasant setting close to the city.

Tent pitches, caravan parking, and rental rooms are available.

Prices for tent pitches vary between CHF 25 and CHF 40 per night, depending on the season and location within the campsite.

It's critical to check the websites of individual campsites or contact them directly for the most up-to-date price and availability. Furthermore, some campsites may include extra facilities such as swimming pools, restaurants, and recreational activities, which might impact the total cost.

Chapter Six

Switzerland's Nightlife At A Glance

Switzerland has a diversified and active nightlife culture that guarantees fun and the chance to show off your flair. After the sun goes down, there is something for everyone to enjoy, from sophisticated clubs to intimate taverns and cafes.

Trendy nightclubs with globally known DJs can be found in places like Zurich, Geneva, and Basel, where you can dance to throbbing rhythms alongside fashionable residents and visitors. The energy is high, with individuals breaking loose and showing off their skills on the dance floor. Switzerland's pubs and lounges are perfect places to unwind with a drink and mingle on a more leisurely evening. There are plenty of alternatives, whether you want a sophisticated cocktail bar with a panoramic city view or a quaint pub with live music. Switzerland's passion for good wines and spirits offers a diverse range of high-quality drinks to satisfy even the most discriminating palette.

So, if you're looking for a memorable night out, Switzerland's nightlife scene will not disappoint. Prepare to revel in the throbbing atmosphere, flaunt your flair, and make unforgettable memories in this lively European nation.

Guide To Swiss Active Bars And Nightclubs

Switzerland is well-known for its dynamic nightlife, with several busy pubs and nightclubs in major cities. Here is a list of some popular places to go for a vibrant and active nightlife experience:

Zurich City Nightclub and bars

Hive Club: This subterranean club in Zurich's industrial zone attracts famous DJs who perform electronic music on various levels.

Kaufleuten: A chic venue with various bars and dance floors that features a variety of music genres ranging from electronic rhythms to hip-hop and R&B.

Plaza Club: Known for its wide music scene, Plaza Club hosts themed evenings such as reggae, Latin, and techno.

Geneva city Night club and bars

Le Baroque: Located in the center of Geneva, Le Baroque provides a bustling environment with live DJ performances, dancing, and a diverse selection of beverages.

Java Club: Playing a mix of house, hip-hop, and commercial tunes, this trendy nightclub draws a youthful and stylish clientele.

L'Usine: A multi-purpose facility with many venues that accommodate concerts, DJ nights, art exhibits, and other events. L'Usine is well-known for its alternative and underground culture.

Basel city Nightclub and Bars

Nordstern: Nordstern is a famous venue for electronic music fans, hosting both local and international DJs, and is known for its outstanding sound system.

Bar Rouge: Located on the 31st level of the Basel Trade Fair Tower, Bar Rouge provides spectacular views of the city skyline as well as DJs playing a mix of house, R&B, and pop music.

Volkshaus: Throughout the year, Volkshaus, a historic structure renovated into a bustling event venue, organizes a variety of events, concerts, and club nights.

Lausanne City Night Club and Bars

MAD Club: A well-known Lausanne nightclub, MAD Club holds themed events with notable DJs performing electronic, house, and techno music.

D! Club is noted for its cutting-edge music selection, which includes techno, drum & bass, and hip-hop. It is located in the Flon neighborhood.

White Club: With a stylish decor and a variety of music genres, White Club provides a refined partying experience that attracts a broad population.

Remember to double-check each venue's exact schedules, admittance regulations, and dress requirements, since they may differ. It's usually a good idea to prepare ahead of time and, if required, make reservations. Have fun discovering Switzerland's busy pubs and nightclubs!

How to Locate Live Music Venues and Jazz Clubs

Follow these procedures to discover live music venues and jazz bars in Switzerland:

1: Search engines like Google can help you find live music venues and jazz bars in Switzerland. To get relevant results, use phrases such as "live music venues Switzerland" or "jazz bars Switzerland." Investigate several websites and directories that list entertainment places.

2: Check out prominent social media networks such as Facebook, Instagram, and Twitter. Many jazz clubs and music venues have active accounts where they offer event schedules and updates. To find new locations, follow or like the pages of certain venues, or search for relevant hashtags such as #livemusicSwitzerland or #jazzbarsSwitzerland.

3: Local Event Listings: Search for local event listings in Swiss newspapers, journals, and internet platforms. Time Out Switzerland, local city guides, and event aggregator websites often list forthcoming live music and jazz acts.

4: Join online music groups or forums where local performers and music fans may exchange information about live music venues. Websites such as Meetup or Swiss-specific music forums may give information about forthcoming concerts as well as suggestions from other music fans.

5: Interact with locals or ask friends and acquaintances who live in Switzerland for recommendations. They could be familiar with certain live music venues or jazz pubs in the neighborhood. Locals often have firsthand knowledge about lesser-known but high-quality music venues that are not readily accessed online.

6: Explore City areas: While in Switzerland, visit several city areas recognized for their thriving music scenes. Live music and jazz places are popular in Zurich's Langstrasse, Geneva's Quartier des Bains, and Basel's Klybeck Quai. Wander around, seek for signs or posters promoting live music events, and soak up the vibe.

7: Jazz Festivals: Be on the lookout for jazz festivals in Switzerland. These concerts often draw prominent musicians and include a variety of jazz performance locations. Montreux Jazz Festival, Cully Jazz Festival, and Ascona Jazz Festival are a few examples. Schedules and venues may be found on their respective websites.

Remember to double-check venue schedules and availability before visiting, as many may have limited hours or seasonal closures. Enjoy the dynamic Swiss music scene and the country's rich jazz tradition!

Swiss Jazz and Live Music Venues

Switzerland has a thriving live music scene, with various venues showcasing jazz performances. Here are some of Switzerland's most popular live music and jazz venues:

Moods Jazz Club (Zurich): Moods Jazz Club, located in Zurich, is one of Switzerland's most known jazz venues. It features both local and international jazz musicians and a wide spectrum of jazz genres.

Bird's Eye Jazz Club (Basel): Bird's Eye Jazz Club, located in Basel, is a charming venue recognized for its small setting and high-quality jazz performances. It showcases top-class musicians from all around the globe.

Chorus Jazz Club (Lausanne): Lausanne's Chorus Jazz Club is a well-known jazz venue in Switzerland. It features a wide range of jazz genres, from classic to modern, and provides a lively environment for music lovers.

Jazzkantine (Lucerne): Jazzkantine is a well-known jazz venue in Lucerne. It provides regular jazz performances and jam sessions that include both renowned and developing jazz musicians.

Jazz Club L'Étage (Biel/Bienne): Jazz Club L'Étage is a well-known club in Biel/Bienne that features live jazz concerts. It has a broad roster of jazz performers and a pleasant and friendly atmosphere.

Jazzclub Mampf (Frankfurt, Germany - near the Swiss border): Although not in Switzerland, Jazzclub Mampf is worth noting since it is in Frankfurt, Germany, close to the Swiss border. Because of its location, it often hosts prominent jazz performers and draws a Swiss audience.

These are only a few examples of Switzerland's live music and jazz venues. Keep in mind that the music industry is ever-changing, and new venues may open while others may close. To guarantee accurate information, constantly check the most recent schedules and activities.

Tips For A Memorable Night in Swiss

If you want to enjoy a fantastic evening experience in Switzerland, here are some recommendations:

1: Choose the correct city: Switzerland features a number of cities with a thriving nightlife. Zurich, Geneva, Basel, and Lausanne are popular selections since they provide a diverse selection of clubs, pubs, and entertainment places.

2: Before you go out, look into the most popular clubs, pubs, and music venues in the city you're visiting. Look for locations that are recognized for providing live music, DJ performances, or themed events that match your tastes.

3: Dress appropriately: Switzerland's nightlife establishments often have a smart-casual dress requirement. Dressing appropriately will allow you to blend in and acquire entry to elite clubs. Before you travel, find out if any locations have strict dress code requirements.

4: Plan ahead of time: Many clubs have limited seating and may demand reservations or prior ticket sales. Plan your night properly to minimize disappointment and to guarantee that you can get into the locations you wish to see.

5: Explore various scenes: Switzerland has a wide evening environment, so attempt to explore different scenes. There's something for everyone, from fashionable clubs and premium pubs to underground music venues and jazz bars.

5: Engage with locals: Swiss people are typically pleasant, so don't be shy about striking up a discussion with a local. They might propose hidden treasures, lesser-known places, or insider advice to help you make the most of your night out.

7: Public transportation: The public transportation networks in Swiss cities are outstanding. Check the timetables and plan your routes ahead of time to guarantee you can travel about simply and securely, particularly if you want to attend many locations in a single night.

8: Be aware of the drinking age: In Switzerland, the legal drinking age for beer, wine, and spirits is 18 years old. Make sure you have a proper ID with you to confirm your age, since places may request it.

9: Safety first: Prioritize your safety like you would everywhere else. To guarantee a safe and fun nighttime experience, stay in well-lit and populated locations, keep an eye on your valuables, and avoid excessive drinking.

Chapter Seven

Switzerland Food and Drinks

Switzerland is famous for its scrumptious food, which has a beautiful combination of tastes and a broad variety of tasty delicacies. Swiss gastronomy never fails to delight the taste senses, from rich and creamy cheeses like Gruyère and Emmental to luscious chocolate concoctions.

The gastronomic landscape of Switzerland is distinguished by its excellent quality and attention to detail. The country's world-famous Swiss chocolate is a veritable masterpiece, with a velvety texture and the ideal sweetness balance. A taste of Swiss chocolate is like listening to a symphony of flavors dance on your tongue. Aside from chocolate, Swiss cuisine has a variety of gastronomic treats. Traditional meals like fondue and raclette highlight the country's great cheese-making ability, providing a divine mix of gooey, melted cheese and crusty bread. The Swiss are also proud of their wonderful pastries, such as buttery and flaky croissants and the divine hazelnut-filled Nusstorte.

Switzerland has an outstanding assortment of beverages to compliment its gastronomic pleasures. Swiss wines are earning worldwide acclaim, with clean whites and powerful reds enthralling wine enthusiasts. The delicious Alpine spring water in the nation is known for its cleanliness and is often consumed directly from the source.

Finally, the cuisine and beverages of Switzerland enchant with their extraordinary richness, rich tastes, and unmistakable deliciousness. Exploring this lovely country's numerous gastronomic options is a great joy for any foodie.

Favorite Swiss Food And Cuisines

Switzerland is well-known for its varied culinary traditions, which have been inspired by surrounding nations such as France, Germany, and Italy. Here are some of the most popular meals and cuisines in Switzerland:

Cheese Fondue: A traditional Swiss meal, cheese fondue is produced by melting a variety of Swiss cheeses, including Gruyère and Emmental, with garlic and white wine. It is generally served with bread pieces for dipping.

Raclette: Raclette is another classic Swiss cheese meal that consists of melting a wheel of raclette cheese then scraping the melted cheese over boiling potatoes, pickles, and onions. It is popular throughout the winter months.

Rösti is a kind of Swiss potato pancake made from shredded potatoes. It is often fried till crispy and served as a side dish or as a main entrée, frequently topped with cheese, bacon, or fried eggs.

Zürcher Geschnetzeltes: A Zurich delicacy consisting of sliced veal stewed in a creamy white wine and mushroom sauce. It's usually served with rösti.

Fondue Chinoise: Fondue Chinoise is a classic holiday and celebration meal that includes cooking thin slices of meat, generally beef or chicken, in a savory broth. After that, the cooked meat is dipped in different sauces.

Swiss Chocolate: Switzerland is well-known for producing high-quality chocolate. Swiss chocolate is distinguished by its smooth texture, rich tastes, and utilization of high-quality ingredients. Lindt, Toblerone, and Nestlé are some well-known Swiss chocolate brands.

Zürcher Eintopf is a substantial Zurich-style stew cooked with beef, vegetables (such as potatoes, carrots, and leeks), and a variety of herbs and spices. It's a hearty and tasty dinner.

Swiss Pastries: Buttery croissants, pain au chocolat (chocolate-filled croissants), Nusstorte (traditional Engadine nut pie), and Basler Läckerli (spiced honey biscuits) are among the excellent pastries available in Switzerland.

Swiss Alps Cuisine: Alpine macaroni (pasta with cheese, cream, and onions), (a meal similar to macaroni and cheese, but with extra potatoes and onions), and other game meats like deer and ibex may be found in the Swiss Alps.

Swiss Wines: Switzerland is known for its superb wines, which include white wines from the Valais area and red wines from the canton of Ticino. Swiss wines are often paired with meals, notably fondue and raclette.

These are just a few examples of popular Swiss meals and cuisines. The nation has a diverse culinary legacy with something to please every palate.

Switzerland Favorite Drinks

Switzerland is well-known for its wide variety of alcoholic and non-alcoholic drinks. Here are a few of the Swiss' favorite beverages:

Coffee: The Swiss adore their coffee. Coffeehouses and cafés are prevalent across Switzerland, providing a range of coffee alternatives such as espresso, cappuccino, and latte.

Hot Chocolate: Swiss hot chocolate is famous for its rich, creamy flavor. It is often served with whipped cream and contains actual melted chocolate.

Mineral Water: Switzerland is well-known for its pure Alpine water. Bottled mineral water is extensively drunk and comes in a variety of brands.

Beer: Locals and tourists alike like Swiss beer. There are several breweries around the nation, serving a variety of varieties such as lagers, ales, and wheat beers.

Wine: Switzerland produces a lot of wine, and each area has its own peculiarities. Swiss wines are noted for their high quality and variety, with white, red, and rosé kinds available.

Cider: Cider is a popular beverage in certain parts of Switzerland, particularly in the French-speaking area. Swiss cider is often prepared from apples cultivated locally and has a crisp, refreshing flavor.

Rivella is a one-of-a-kind Swiss soft drink manufactured from whey, a byproduct of cheese manufacturing. It has a unique taste and comes in many varieties, including Rivella Red (normal) and Rivella Blue (sugar-free).

Aperol Spritz: This iconic Italian aperitif is also becoming popular in Switzerland. It's made up of Aperol, Prosecco, and soda water, and it's served over ice with an orange slice.

Herbal Infusions: Swiss people enjoy a wide range of herbal infusions or herbal teas, which are often produced from locally obtained herbs and flowers. These infusions are well-known for their calming and rejuvenating properties.

Absinthe: While not as popular as the other beverages on our list, absinthe has historical importance in Switzerland. It is an anise-flavored liquor with a high alcohol level that is generally diluted with water and sugar before use.

These are just a few examples of popular beverages in Switzerland. Beverage tastes may differ based on area and personal preference.

Swiss Vegan And Vegetarian Options

In recent years, Switzerland, like many other nations, has experienced an upsurge in the availability of vegetarian and vegan alternatives. Here are some possibilities for vegetarians and vegans in Switzerland:

Restaurants and Cafés: Many Swiss restaurants and cafés now have vegetarian and vegan food on their menus. Salads and soups, as well as plant-based burgers, pizzas, and pastas, are all available. Hiltl in Zurich (the world's oldest vegetarian restaurant), Tibits with many locations, and Vegelateria in Geneva are some popular vegetarian and vegan restaurants in Switzerland.

Health Food shops: Switzerland offers a number of health food shops that sell a variety of vegetarian and vegan items. These shops sell meat and dairy alternatives such as plant-based milks, cheeses, and meat replacements.

Alnatura, Coop Vitality, and Denn's Biomarkt are some well-known health food shops in Switzerland.

Farmers Markets: Farmers markets are an excellent source of fresh, locally produced vegetables as well as vegetarian items. Farmers markets may be found across Switzerland, where you can buy fruits, vegetables, grains, and other plant-based items directly from local farmers and producers. It's a great way to support local farmers while still enjoying fresh, organic products.

Online Delivery Services: As online delivery services have grown in popularity, it has become simpler to find vegetarian and vegan items in Switzerland. Websites and applications like Farmy, LeShop, and Coop@Home provide a diverse range of plant-based foods that may be delivered to your home.

Vegan-Friendly Cities: Some Swiss cities are well-known for their vegan-friendliness. Vegetarian and vegan restaurants, cafés, and shops are more prevalent in Zurich, Basel, Geneva, and Lausanne, for example. These cities often offer vegan festivals and events, increasing the number of plant-based eating alternatives.

When eating out, remember to examine the ingredients and inquire about cooking techniques to verify that the foods are compatible for your dietary needs. Furthermore, informing the staff about your dietary limitations is usually beneficial so that they may direct you to appropriate selections or make required arrangements.

Best Cafes & Restaurants in Switzerland

Switzerland is famed for its culinary prowess, with a diverse assortment of cafés and restaurants catering to a variety of tastes and preferences. Here are a few of the top cafés and restaurants in Switzerland:

Café de l'Horloge (Geneva): This beautiful café with outside seating is located in the center of Geneva. They provide delectable pastries and desserts, as well as a range of hot and cold drinks.

Zeughauskeller (Zurich): This ancient Zurich restaurant is well-known for its classic Swiss food. Hearty foods like veal sausage, rösti (Swiss-style grated and fried potatoes), and fondue are available. The restaurant is located in an old arsenal, which adds to the restaurant's distinctive ambience.

Sprüngli (Zürich): Sprüngli is a well-known Swiss café and chocolatier known for its high-quality chocolates and pastries. Their Zurich flagship shop has a great range of sweets as well as a café where you can sample their distinctive hot chocolate and pastries.

Café du Soleil (Geneva): One of the city's oldest eateries, Café du Soleil is located in the lovely old town of Geneva. It specializes in classic Swiss cuisine like raclette and fondue, which are made using high-quality local ingredients.

Brasserie Lipp (Geneva): Brasserie Lipp is a typical French brasserie in Geneva's center. It serves a variety of French meals, including escargots, steak frites, and a large selection of seafood. The beautiful and energetic environment of the restaurant enhances the whole eating experience.

Kronenhalle (Zurich): The Kronenhalle is a famed Zurich restaurant noted for its excellent Swiss cuisine as well as its magnificent art collection. For decades, it has been a favorite of painters, authors, and intellectuals. Classics on the menu include Zürcher Geschnetzeltes (sliced veal in a creamy sauce) and Wiener Schnitzel.

Kornhauskeller (Bern): Kornhauskeller, located in a historic building in Bern, provides a unique eating experience in a picturesque environment. The restaurant provides classic Swiss and Mediterranean cuisine, and the subterranean bar is a popular hangout for beverages and live music.

Hiltl (Zurich): Hiltl, founded in 1898, is the world's oldest vegetarian restaurant. It serves a varied selection of vegetarian and vegan meals from across the world. There is also a stylish bar and lounge area inside the restaurant.

These are just a handful of the amazing cafés and restaurants available in Switzerland. You'll have lots of opportunities to discover and appreciate the country's culinary culture throughout your vacation.

Switzerland Dining Etiquette

Because Switzerland is a bilingual and multicultural nation, dining etiquette is influenced by both French and German customs. Here are some important things to remember while eating in Switzerland:

1: Punctuality: Swiss people place a high emphasis on punctuality, therefore it's essential to be on time for a dinner reservation. Being fashionably late is typically frowned upon.

2: When entering a restaurant or someone's house, it is usual to shake hands with the host or hostess and say "Guten Tag" (Good day) or "Grüezi" (a Swiss German greeting).

3: Table manners: Good table manners are valued in Swiss dining etiquette. Maintain visibility of your hands on the table, but not of your elbows. It is customary to wait until everyone has been served before commencing to eat. Remember to chew with your mouth closed and to avoid chatting while eating.

4: Silverware usage: The Swiss use silverware in the continental European manner. Hold the fork in your left hand and the knife in your right. After cutting a portion of food, set the knife on the plate's edge with the blade pointing inwards and eat with your right hand.

5: Maintain eye contact and clink glasses with everyone at the table while toasting. Before taking a drink, say "Prost"

(German) or "Santé" (French). During a toast, it is usual to consume your drink in one gulp.

6: Tipping: Although service costs are normally included in the bill in Switzerland, it is customary to offer a little gratuity as a token of gratitude. If you're pleased with the service, round up the sum or add an extra 5-10%.

7: Cheese etiquette: Switzerland is famed for its cheese, and it's necessary to know basic cheese etiquette while eating in a Swiss context. To prevent taste mingling, use a different knife for each cheese. Swiss cheese is often eaten with bread and not on the same plate with other dishes such as fruits or meats.

8: Language: The official languages of Switzerland are German, French, Italian, and Romansh. The language spoken may differ depending on the locale. If you're uncertain, address the staff and other visitors in their native tongue or in English.

Remember that these are broad rules, and there may be some differences based on the location or institution. A nice eating experience in Switzerland will be ensured by adhering to and respecting local customs and traditions.

Chapter Eight

What To Know As A First Time Visitor Before Your Visit To Switzerland

Tourists must be aware of important Switzerland travel guidelines before embarking on their journey. Switzerland is a famous tourist destination due to its various landscapes, which include the Alps and lovely towns.

About Swiss Currency

The Swiss franc (CHF) is the country's currency. The franc is the official currency of Switzerland and Liechtenstein, and it is also used in Campione d'Italia, an Italian exclave. The Swiss franc is abbreviated as CHF, which stands for "Confoederatio Helvetica Franc," the Latin name for Switzerland.

The Swiss franc is a highly appreciated currency that is often viewed as a safe-haven currency, which means that its value tends to hold or increase during periods of global economic turmoil. It is widely recognized in Switzerland and may be used for a variety of transactions such as shopping, eating, and transportation.

In Switzerland, banknotes come in denominations of 10, 20, 50, 100, 200, and 1,000 francs, while coins come in 5, 10, 20, and 50 centimes, as well as 1, 2, and 5 francs. The Swiss National Bank (SNB) issues and regulates the currency and is in charge of preserving price stability and the general economic well-being of Switzerland.

When exchanging money or making purchases in Switzerland, keep in mind that the nation is not a member of the European Union, hence the euro is not frequently recognised as legal cash. Some stores near the borders may take euros, but it's generally a good idea to have Swiss francs on hand for most transactions.

If you want to convert your cash into Swiss francs, you must keep an eye on the exchange rates, since they might vary. Furthermore, since Switzerland is recognized for its high cost of living, pricing for products and services may be higher in comparison to other nations.

Money Exchange Spot In Switzerland

In Switzerland, you may exchange money at a variety of locations. Here are some typical alternatives:

Banks: Swiss banks provide currency exchange services and may be used to convert money at their branches. This service is provided by major banks such as UBS, Credit Suisse, and PostFinance.

Currency Exchange Offices: Currency exchange offices are available in major towns and tourist destinations across Switzerland. These offices often provide competitive rates and may have longer hours than banks.

Airports and large railway stations in Switzerland often include currency exchange desks or kiosks where you may exchange money. However, keep in mind that the exchange rates may not be as good as other possibilities.

Post Offices: Swiss post offices provide currency exchange services as well. Most towns and cities have post offices, and they usually provide reasonable prices.

Hotels may provide currency exchange services to its visitors. However, the rates may not be as attractive, so compare them to other possibilities before making a selection.

Internet Currency Exchanges: You may swap money digitally using internet platforms and mobile applications. These platforms often provide cheap rates and easy transactions. However, be certain that you choose a reliable and secure provider.

To obtain the greatest bargain while converting money, check rates and fees at several locations or platforms. Be aware of any possible service fees, commissions, or minimum exchange amounts that may apply.

Consider Travel Insurance

When planning a vacation to Switzerland, it is a good idea to have travel insurance. Travel insurance protects you against unexpected incidents that may occur before or during your journey. Here are some of the reasons why travel insurance might be useful while visiting Switzerland:

Vacation Cancellation or Interruption: If you have to cancel or cut short your vacation due to covered causes such as sickness, injury, or unanticipated problems, travel insurance may compensate you for non-refundable charges. This may assist safeguard your investment in the event of unforeseen situations.

Medical Emergencies: While Switzerland offers outstanding healthcare facilities, medical charges for tourists may be expensive. If necessary, travel insurance may cover emergency medical bills, hospitalization, and medical evacuation. It is critical to evaluate the coverage limitations to ensure they are enough for your requirements.

Baggage Loss or Delay: Travel insurance may cover baggage that is lost, stolen, or delayed. If your baggage is lost or delayed, travel insurance may pay you for necessary purchases made during your trip.

Travel Delays or Cancellations: If your flights or other modes of transportation are delayed or canceled, travel insurance may compensate you for extra expenditures such as lodging, food, and other transit arrangements.

Personal Liability: Travel insurance may provide personal liability coverage in the event that you cause property damage or harm someone while vacationing in Switzerland.

It is critical to thoroughly research the policy conditions, coverage limitations, exclusions, and any extra alternatives available before acquiring travel insurance. Consider your personal requirements as well as the activities you want to participate in while in Switzerland, like skiing or adventure sports, since they may need extra coverage.

It's also worth mentioning that some credit cards provide travel insurance advantages, so see if yours does before getting a separate policy. To understand the degree of protection provided by your credit card coverage, always read the terms and restrictions.

Remember that travel insurance is intended to offer you peace of mind as well as financial security throughout your vacation. To choose the policy that best meets your requirements and budget, it is advised that you evaluate several insurance companies, their coverage choices, and rates.

LGBTQ + Acceptance

When planning a vacation to Switzerland, it is a good idea to have travel insurance. Travel insurance protects you against unexpected incidents that may occur before or during your journey. Here are some of the reasons why travel insurance might be useful while visiting Switzerland:

Vacation Cancellation or Interruption: If you have to cancel or cut short your vacation due to covered causes such as sickness, injury, or unanticipated problems, travel insurance may compensate you for non-refundable charges. This may assist safeguard your investment in the event of unforeseen situations.

Medical Emergencies: While Switzerland offers outstanding healthcare facilities, medical charges for tourists may be expensive. If necessary, travel insurance may cover emergency medical bills, hospitalization, and medical evacuation. It is critical to evaluate the coverage limitations to ensure they are enough for your requirements.

Baggage Loss or Delay: Travel insurance may cover baggage that is lost, stolen, or delayed. If your baggage is lost or delayed, travel insurance may pay you for necessary purchases made during your trip.

Travel Delays or Cancellations: If your flights or other modes of transportation are delayed or canceled, travel insurance may compensate you for extra expenditures such as lodging, food, and other transit arrangements.

Personal Liability: Travel insurance may provide personal liability coverage in the event that you cause property damage or harm someone while vacationing in Switzerland.

It is critical to thoroughly research the policy conditions, coverage limitations, exclusions, and any extra alternatives available before acquiring travel insurance. Consider your personal requirements as well as the activities you want to participate in while in Switzerland, like skiing or adventure sports, since they may need extra coverage.

It's also worth mentioning that some credit cards provide travel insurance advantages, so see if yours does before getting a separate policy. To understand the degree of protection provided by your credit card coverage, always read the terms and restrictions.

Remember that travel insurance is intended to offer you peace of mind as well as financial security throughout your vacation. To choose the policy that best meets your requirements and budget, it is advised that you evaluate several insurance companies, their coverage choices, and rates.

Emergency Contacts

The following are the emergency contact numbers in Switzerland:

112 or 117 for emergency services

In the event of a life-threatening emergency, such as a fire, major accident, or medical emergency, dial 112 or 117.
117 police officers

Dial 117 to reach the Swiss police in non-emergency circumstances that need police help.
144 ambulances and medical emergencies

In the event of a medical emergency or if you need urgent medical help, dial 144 to contact emergency medical services (ambulance).
118th Fire Department

In the event of a fire or a fire-related emergency, dial 118 to call the fire department.
145 Poison Control Center

If you suspect poisoning or need guidance on dangerous chemicals, dial 145.
Touring Club Switzerland Road Assistance: 140

If you need roadside assistance or assistance with your car, call the Touring Club Switzerland at 140.

Please keep in mind that all emergency contact numbers are current as of my knowledge cutoff date of September 2021. However, it's always a good idea to double-check for the most recent emergency contact information in case anything has changed since then.

Switzerland Cultural Etiquette

Switzerland is well-known for its numerous cultural influences, which include German, French, Italian, and

Romansh traditions. Here are some cultural etiquette standards to remember while visiting or engaging with Swiss people:

1; Timeliness: The Swiss put a high value on timeliness. On-time arrival for appointments, meetings, and social gatherings is highly valued. It is generally impolite to keep people waiting, so organize your itinerary properly.

2: Greetings: It is usual to shake hands and establish eye contact while meeting someone new. Use a formal welcome like "Guten Tag" or "Grüezi" (a typical Swiss German greeting). Close friends and family members may share cheek kisses.

3: Swiss has four official languages: German, French, Italian, and Romansh. Because the language spoken in each place differs, it is courteous to enquire about the preferred language of communication. English is widely known and spoken across the country, particularly in tourist regions.

4: Respect personal space: Because Swiss people appreciate their privacy, it is essential to maintain an acceptable physical distance while communicating. Unless you have a strong connection with someone, avoid excessive touching or standing too near to them.

5: Dining etiquette: It is normal to bring a little present for the host, like flowers or a box of chocolates, when invited to someone's house for dinner. Allow the host to begin the meal and then follow their example in terms of table etiquette. It is expected that you finish everything on your plate.

6: Tipping: Although service charges are often included in restaurant bills, it is customary to round up the amount or give a little tip as a token of gratitude for excellent service. Small change as a tip is often appreciated at cafés and pubs.

7: Recycling and sanitation: Switzerland is well-known for its stringent recycling rules. Make careful you segregate and dispose of garbage in accordance with local regulations. Littering is also frowned upon, thus public places must be kept clean and orderly.

8: Formality: In commercial and social contexts, Swiss culture is formal. Unless they indicate differently, address someone by their last name. Follow the last name with "Her" for Mr. and "Frau" for Mrs./Ms. Once you've established a connection, you may start utilizing first names.

9: Direct communication: The Swiss value direct and simple communication. They admire clarity and honesty, so rather than using ambiguity, communicate your views and opinions freely.

10: Dress code: Switzerland has a modest dress code in general, especially in business and professional settings. Unless you are in a very casual atmosphere, it is advisable to dress appropriately and avoid wearing anything too casual or revealing.

Remember that these are general suggestions that may vary depending on geographical area or individual tastes. Following these cultural etiquette guidelines can help you create a good impression and respect Swiss customs and traditions.

Chapter Nine

Swiss Travel Budget And Financial Management

For travelers considering a vacation to Switzerland, financial management and preparation are essential. Switzerland is well-known for its high living costs and pricey tourism attractions. Tourists may ensure they have enough money for lodging, transportation, food, and activities by carefully managing and arranging their spending. Setting a budget, researching cost-effective choices, comparing costs, and making educated selections to maximize their trip experience while keeping within their financial means are all part of this process.

Swiss Money Saving Strategies

Switzerland is famed for its beautiful scenery, top-quality services, and, sadly, expensive pricing. You can, however, make the most of your vacation to Switzerland without breaking the bank with a little forethought and some clever money-saving suggestions. Here are some of the best money-saving suggestions for travelers visiting Switzerland:

1: Off-season travel: Switzerland may be fairly pricey during high tourist seasons. Consider coming during shoulder or off-peak seasons, such as spring or fall, when hotel and airfare rates are often cheaper.

2: Instead of staying in luxury hotels, try staying in budget-friendly options such as guesthouses, hostels, or vacation rentals. Websites such as Airbnb and Booking.com provide a large selection of low-cost rooms.

3: Use public transit: Switzerland has a fantastic public transportation system that includes trains, buses, and boats. To enjoy unrestricted travel throughout your stay, get a Swiss Travel Pass or a regional transit card. This may be less expensive than hiring a vehicle or buying individual tickets.

4: Pack your own lunch: Eating out in Switzerland may be costly, so save money by bringing your own lunch on day excursions. Migros and Coop supermarkets provide a wide range of fresh and cheap food alternatives. Consider taking a picnic in the gorgeous Swiss countryside.

5: Discover free attractions and activities: Switzerland is well-known for its natural beauty, and many of its attractions are either free or affordable. Outdoor activities may be enjoyed in hiking routes, public parks, and lakes. Look for free entrance days or cheap tickets to museums.

6: Drink tap water: Switzerland has great tap water quality, so instead of purchasing bottled water, bring a reusable water bottle with you and fill it up at the tap. This simple change may save you a substantial amount of money throughout your vacation.

7: Take use of free public facilities: Switzerland provides a number of free public amenities to tourists. Many cities and towns provide free public bathrooms, Wi-Fi hotspots, and drinking fountains.

8: Consider getting a half-priced card: If you intend to use public transit often, the Swiss Half Fare Card may save you money on train, bus, and boat tickets. It provides a 50% discount on the majority of public transportation services.

9: Souvenir stores in tourist locations are notorious for charging exorbitant rates. Instead, explore for local markets, artisanal stores, or tiny villages where you may discover true Swiss goods at a lower cost.

10: Plan and book ahead of time: Booking lodgings, transportation, and activities ahead of time generally results in better bargains and discounts. To save money, compare rates and take advantage of early-bird specials.

Remember that, although Switzerland might be an expensive destination, you can still enjoy its beauty on a budget. You may enjoy a wonderful vacation without overpaying if you follow these money-saving suggestions.

Bargaining and Negotiation Strategies

When haggling and negotiating with Swiss marketers as a tourist, keep a few crucial points in mind to achieve a good end. Here are a few ideas:

Gather information and perform research: Before participating in any discussions, undertake extensive study on the product or service you're interested in acquiring. Understand its market worth, average price, and any local negotiating norms or practices.

Respectfully approach negotiations: Swiss society appreciates civility and professionalism. When dealing with marketers, be friendly, courteous, and respectful. Maintain a nice tone during negotiations and avoid employing aggressive or confrontational techniques.

Know your budget and priorities: Establish a budget and prioritize the areas that are most important to you. This will allow you to make more informed judgments during negotiations and highlight areas where you may make concessions or seek better agreements.

Be patient and prepared to walk away: Bargaining may not be as common in Switzerland as it is in other nations. Some marketers may have predetermined rates or only allow for a limited amount of bargaining. If you face opposition or find the pricing unnegotiable, be prepared to gracefully go if it fails to match your expectations.

Consider additional variables that might add value to your purchase in addition to price while bargaining. Additional services, extended warranties, or packaged offerings may be included. Sometimes the complete bundle is more valuable than just obtaining a reduced price.

Employ courteous negotiating approaches such as asking open-ended questions, requesting clarification, and exhibiting genuine curiosity. This strategy may encourage constructive discourse and boost your chances of achieving a mutually beneficial arrangement.

Consider local traditions and language: Learn the basics of local customs and, if feasible, a few words in the local language. This effort shows your appreciation for the local culture and may contribute to a more favorable bargaining climate.

Seek advice from locals: If you're unsure about local practices or need help negotiating, don't be afraid to ask locals or hotel personnel for help. They may give vital insights and assist you in efficiently navigating the negotiating process.

Remember that negotiating results might differ based on the circumstances and the person in question. When dealing with Swiss marketers as a tourist, you boost your chances of a satisfactory conclusion by approaching talks with respect, preparedness, and a pleasant attitude.

Top Switzerland Budget Markets

Switzerland is well-known for its high level of life and is sometimes seen as an expensive place to live. There are, however, budget-friendly marketplaces where you may get moderately priced things. Here are some of Switzerland's biggest budget markets:

Lidl: Lidl is a prominent discount grocery company that sells a broad variety of low-cost food, home goods, and other necessities. They have many sites around Switzerland and are well-known for their low costs.

Aldi: Another well-known cheap grocery business that provides low-cost foods such as fresh fruit, meat, and dairy items is Aldi. They have a presence in various Swiss cities and are a good alternative for those on a tight budget.

Denner is a Swiss cheap grocery business that provides a wide range of items at lower rates than other supermarkets. They sell a wide range of food, drinks, and home products.

Migros Outlet: Migros is one of Switzerland's leading grocery chains, and they offer outlet locations where you can get reduced merchandise. These stores sell a variety of commodities at discounted costs, including food, apparel, electronics, and home goods.

Coop Pronto: Coop Pronto is a Swiss convenience store chain that sells groceries, snacks, and other daily products. While convenience shops are often more costly than traditional supermarkets, Coop Pronto frequently provides specials and deals that might make it a more cost-effective alternative.

Flea Markets: Switzerland offers various flea markets where you may discover inexpensive used products, antiques, clothes, and other stuff. These markets, such as Zurich's Bürkliplatz Flea Market or Geneva's Plainpalais Flea Market, are ideal for bargain seekers hunting for one-of-a-kind items.

It's worth noting that, although some marketplaces provide more cheap selections than other retailers in Switzerland, prices may still be higher than in other nations. Nonetheless, they might be an excellent way to save money when shopping in Switzerland.

Chapter Ten

Goodbye, Switzerland

As we complete our travel guide, we say goodbye to Switzerland, a mesmerizing country that has left an unforgettable impact on the hearts and minds of everyone who has had the pleasure of visiting. Each city provided a distinct perspective on Swiss life, fusing history and modernity in ways that only Switzerland can.

Switzerland has an unrivaled reputation for accuracy, craftsmanship, and innovation, in addition to its physical beauty and cultural richness. It is a country that has given the world revolutionary innovations, such as the Swiss Army Knife and the Swiss watchmaking heritage, which has become associated with accuracy and workmanship. Switzerland's drive to excellence is evident in its school system, healthcare system, and commitment to environmental sustainability, making it a model for nations across the world.

Guide To Swiss Souvenirs

Switzerland is well-known for its breathtaking scenery, delectable chocolates, magnificent timepieces, and high-quality Swiss army knives. When it comes to souvenirs from Switzerland, the following are popular selections among tourists:

Swiss Chocolate: Switzerland is well-known for producing world-class chocolate. Look for well-known brands such as Lindt, Toblerone, and Sprüngli, and think about purchasing chocolate bars, truffles, or pralines as mementos.

Swiss Watches: Switzerland is well-known for its watchmaking accuracy and artistry. Consider buying a Swiss watch as a unique and timeless gift. Rolex, TAG Heuer, and Omega are well-known brands.

Swiss Army Knife: A Swiss army knife is a multi-purpose instrument that includes blades, scissors, screwdrivers, and other tools. The most popular brands of real Swiss army knives are Victorinox and Wenger.

Swiss Cowbells: The lovely landscapes of Switzerland are often linked with grazing cows ornamented with cowbells.

These classic cowbells are wonderful keepsakes and come in a variety of sizes and styles.

Swiss Cheese: Switzerland is famous for its wonderful cheeses including Emmental, Gruyère, and Appenzeller. As a keepsake, consider purchasing a wheel or smaller chunks of these cheeses. They are usually vacuum-sealed for ease of shipping.

Swiss Handicrafts: Switzerland is well-known for its traditional arts and crafts. Look for objects made of wood that have been created, such as cuckoo clocks, music boxes, or beautiful carvings. Other distinctive souvenirs include traditional Swiss fabrics, needlework, and ceramics.

Swiss Alps Memorabilia: When visiting the Swiss Alps, you may purchase a variety of souvenirs connected to mountain sports and activities. Look for ski souvenirs, mountain-themed clothes, or accessories depicting famous mountain peaks such as the Matterhorn or Jungfrau.

Postcards and magnets showing renowned Swiss monuments, stunning landscapes, or cultural icons are popular and affordable gifts that may be found at gift stores.

Remember to verify your home country's customs procedures and limitations before buying any food goods or anything derived from animal resources. Explore local markets, gift shops, and department stores for a broad range of mementos that reflect the character of your Swiss journey.

Safety Tips For First-Time Visitors

If you're a first-time tourist to Switzerland, it's critical to prioritize your safety. Switzerland is typically a secure nation with low crime rates, but taking measures and being prepared is always a good idea. Here are some safety recommendations and ideas for your visit:

- Research and plan: Before your journey, get acquainted with the locations you want to visit. Discover local traditions, legislation, and emergency contact information. Examine the most recent COVID-19 recommendations as well as any travel advisories or warnings for the particular locations you'll be visiting.

- While Switzerland is regarded as secure, it is nevertheless vital to stay attentive and aware of your surroundings, particularly in popular tourist locations or on public transit. Keep an eye on your possessions at all times and avoid exhibiting important goods publicly.

- Secure your belongings: Although Switzerland has a low crime rate, petty theft may occur, especially in tourist areas. Keep valuables such as passports, cash, and electronic gadgets in a secure location, such as a hotel safe. When you're out and about, keep a secure bag or backpack near to your body.

- Follow traffic rules: If you want to drive in Switzerland, be informed of the local traffic restrictions and closely adhere to them. Because Swiss roads may be small and twisting, drive carefully and within speed restrictions. If you use public transit, be aware of boarding and departure procedures, as well as any safety announcements.

- Nature and outdoor activities should be respected: Switzerland is recognized for its beautiful landscapes and outdoor activities. If you're going hiking, skiing, or doing other outdoor activities, be sure you have the proper clothing and equipment. Follow safety instructions and familiarize yourself with the path or activity difficulty level. Avoid dangerous conduct and be aware of changing weather conditions.

- Be prepared for weather changes: Even in the summer, the weather in Switzerland may be unpredictable. Layer your clothes to accommodate temperature variations, and always have a rain jacket or umbrella. Check the weather forecast ahead of time and be prepared for rapid weather changes if you're planning outside activities.

- Use licensed guides or tour operators: If you're doing guided activities like climbing or skiing, be sure the guides or tour operators are licensed and trustworthy. They will have the experience and knowledge essential to assure your safety throughout these activities.

- Be careful while engaging in outdoor water activities: Switzerland offers several lakes and rivers where you may engage in water activities. Be careful, though, and be mindful of any currents, tides, or prohibited places. Always swim in approved areas, obey any safety warnings or instructions, and, if required, use a life jacket.

- Stay connected and informed: Always have your phone charged and a method of contact with you. To remain connected, consider purchasing a local SIM card or an international data package. Maintain awareness of any local developments or crises by following news and public pronouncements.

Remember that, although taking these measures is essential, it is also critical to enjoy your vacation and make the most of your time in Switzerland. Stay prepared, exercise common sense, and have a fantastic time visiting the country's stunning scenery and diverse culture.

Helpful Websites and Booking Resources

There are various reputable booking services and information for Switzerland that may assist you in properly planning your trip. Here are a few examples:

Booking.com (*www.booking.com*): *This* website provides a variety of lodging alternatives, such as hotels, flats, and guesthouses. It offers user reviews, flexible search options, and reasonable costs.

Expedia (*www.expedia.com*): Expedia is a popular online travel service where you can book flights, hotels, holiday packages, and car rentals. It often provides specials and discounts, making it an excellent choice for budget-conscious visitors.

Airbnb (*www.airbnb.com*): *Airbnb* is a popular option for staying in unusual lodgings such as private homes, flats, or even treehouses. It provides a choice of selections at various pricing points, as well as guest reviews and verified listings.

Swiss Travel System (*www.swiss-pass.ch*): If you want to travel widely in Switzerland by public transportation, the Swiss Travel System website is a helpful resource. The Swiss Travel Pass, which allows unrestricted travel on trains, buses, and boats across the nation, may be purchased.

SBB (*www.sbb.ch*): The Swiss Federal Railways' official website. It lets you look for rail connections, check timetables, and buy tickets for internal and international travel inside Switzerland.

Swiss tourist (*www.myswitzerland.com*): Switzerland's official tourist website offers detailed information on popular destinations, sites, activities, and events around the country. It provides travel advice, recommended itineraries, and resources to assist you in planning your trip.

TripAdvisor (*www.tripadvisor.com*): TripAdvisor is a trustworthy site for discovering reviews, suggestions, and travel advice from other travelers. It provides a broad variety of travel-related information in Switzerland, such as hotels, sights, restaurants, and activities.

Before making your final reservations, remember to compare costs and check several sources. It's also a good idea to read reviews and do research to ensure that the selected hotel or service fulfills your expectations.

7 Days Itinerary In Switzerland

DAY 1

Morning: When you arrive in Zurich, check into your hotel.

Visit the Grossmünster, Fraumünster, and the Bahnhofstrasse retail area on a walking tour of Zurich's old town.

Price: Prices for walking tours vary, but expect to spend between $25 and $30.

Afternoon: Visit the Kunsthaus Zurich, a world-famous art museum with a broad collection of modern and contemporary art.

The admission fee is roughly $20.

Evening: Dinner in a classic Swiss restaurant, where you may sample local favorites like fondue or raclette.

Price: Prices vary per restaurant, but expect to pay between $40 and $50 for a dinner.

DAY 2

Morning: Travel by rail to Lucerne (around 1 hour from Zurich).

Wander around the lovely old town and see the renowned Chapel Bridge.

Train ticket rates vary, but a round-trip ticket should cost roughly $30-40.

Afternoon: Take a boat ride on Lake Lucerne, savoring the beautiful scenery and stopping at the lovely hamlet of Vitznau.

Boat trips cost between $30 and $40.

Evening: Enjoy a leisurely evening walk along the lake promenade while admiring the stunning sights.

Consider eating at a lakefront restaurant.

Price: Prices vary per restaurant, but expect to pay between $40 and $50 for a dinner.

DAY 3

Morning: Travel by rail to Interlaken (around 2 hours from Lucerne).

Visit the Höhematte Park for panoramic views of the surrounding mountains and explore the city core.

Price: Train tickets vary in price, but expect to spend between $50 and $60 for a round-trip ticket.

Afternoon: Take a cable car to the Schilthorn top for panoramic views of the Swiss Alps.

The cost of a cable car ticket is between $60 and $70.

Evening: A supper presentation involving music, dance, and local traditions will introduce you to authentic Swiss culture.

Dinner show tickets vary, but plan to spend between $70-80.

Day 4

Morning: Travel by rail to Zermatt (about 2.5 hours from Interlaken).

Explore the car-free hamlet, stroll along the main street, and pay a visit to the Matterhorn Museum.

Price: Train tickets vary in price, but a round-trip ticket should cost approximately $80-90.

Afternoon: Take the Gornergrat Bahn, a cogwheel train that will take you to the Gornergrat top for spectacular views of the Matterhorn and neighboring peaks.

The cost of a train ticket is between $80-90.

Evening: Enjoy a classic Swiss meal in a quaint Zermatt restaurant, where you may enjoy specialties like raclette or rosti.

Price: Prices vary per restaurant, but expect to pay between $50 and $60 for a dinner.

Day 5

Morning: Travel by rail to Geneva (around 4 hours from Zermatt).
Explore the Palais des Nations and the United Nations Office on a guided tour.
Price: Guided tours begin from $15.

Afternoon: Visit the iconic Jet d'Eau water fountain in Lake Geneva.
Explore the ancient Old Town, which includes St. Pierre Cathedral and the Maison Tavel, Geneva's oldest residence.
The admission to most sites is free.

Evening: Enjoy a gourmet meal at one of Geneva's Michelin-starred restaurants, which are famed for their outstanding food.
Price varies based on the

Day 6

Morning: Travel by rail to Bern (around 1 hour from Geneva).
Discover the UNESCO-listed old town, which includes the Zytglogge (Clock Tower), Bern Cathedral, and Bear Park.

138

Train ticket rates vary, but a round-trip ticket should cost roughly $30-40.

Afternoon: Visit the Paul Klee Center, a museum devoted to the great Swiss painter's works.
The admission fee is roughly $15.

Evening: Take a stroll along the Aare River and lunch at one of the local restaurants serving Swiss specialties.
Price: Prices vary per restaurant, but expect to pay between $40 and $50 for a dinner.

Day 7

Morning: Travel by rail to Lausanne (around 1 hour from Bern).
Learn about the history of the Olympic Games at the Olympic Museum.
The admission fee is roughly $15.

Afternoon: Take a train to Montreux, which is famed for its lovely lakeside setting and the Chillon Castle.
Explore the castle's ancient architecture and rich history.
Admission to the castle costs roughly $15.

Evening: Take in the beautiful sights of the Swiss Riviera on a spectacular dinner cruise on Lake Geneva.

Dinner cruises cost between $50 and $60.

Please keep in mind that the prices shown in this itinerary are estimates and subject to change. Before arranging your vacation, check the current rates and availability. Furthermore, transportation prices may differ based on the kind of ticket, class, and time of travel.

Conclusion

Finally, Switzerland provides an unrivaled travel experience that blends spectacular natural beauty, a rich cultural legacy, and a dedication to quality in all aspects. This travel handbook has delved into the many sides of this fascinating nation, giving detailed information and insights to help you make the most of your trip.

Switzerland's landscapes are a visual feast, from the towering peaks of the Swiss Alps to the tranquil lakes and attractive valleys. Switzerland caters to all inclinations, whether you're an outdoor enthusiast searching for exhilarating experiences like skiing, hiking, or paragliding, or a leisure visitor hoping to unwind among magnificent landscapes. The handbook highlights must-see places like Zurich, Geneva, and Lucerne, where you can immerse yourself in history, culture, and urban pleasures.

Switzerland's dedication to excellence may be seen in its world-famous timepieces, chocolate, and hospitality. The guidebook has offered helpful advice on indulging in these delectable treats, bringing you through luxury shopping districts, charming Swiss chocolatiers, and quiet mountain cabins. Switzerland's culinary culture will leave you wanting more, whether you're eating a delectable fondue or touring the wines of the Lavaux area.

Switzerland's transportation system is efficient and dependable, making it simple to travel the country's many areas. The complete network of railroads, buses, and boats indicated in the handbook ensures smooth transit between cities, mountain resorts, and attractive towns. Furthermore, the Swiss Travel Pass provides convenience and cost advantages for experiencing the nation at your own speed.

The cultural legacy of Switzerland is as lively as its surroundings. The handbook illuminates the country's museums, galleries, and festivals, enabling you to immerse yourself in art, history, and local customs. Whether you're admiring masterpieces at the Kunsthaus Zurich, discovering Bern's ancient old town, or celebrating the Fête de l'Escalade in Geneva, Switzerland's cultural attractions will fascinate your senses.

Finally, Switzerland's dedication to sustainability and environmental protection is admirable. The guidebook stressed the significance of responsible travel, offering eco-friendly suggestions and promoting projects that encourage sustainable tourism. By being attentive of your actions and appreciating Switzerland's natural beauty, you can help to ensure its long-term preservation for future generations.

Finally, Switzerland is a traveler's paradise, delivering a wonderful combination of natural magnificence, cultural richness, and exceptional friendliness. This travel handbook has provided you with the information and advice you need to go on a fantastic vacation across Switzerland, leaving you with lifetime memories of an exquisite nation that really has it all. Pack your luggage, embrace the Swiss character, and be ready to be enchanted by all Switzerland has to offer. Best wishes!

Printed in Great Britain
by Amazon